Kindness IS MY HOBBY

HOW TO CHANGE THE WORLD RIGHT WHERE YOU ARE

Ruby Kate Chitsey

Get Creative 6
NEW YORK

GET CREATIVE 6
An imprint of
Mixed Media Resources
19 W. 21st Street, Suite 601
New York, NY 10010

Editors
TODD HUNTER
PAMELA WISSMAN

Creative Director
IRENE LEDWITH

Book Designer
STACY WAKEFIELD FORTE

Cover photograph by
JOHN DAVID PITTMAN

Interior photographs pages 4,
6, 27, 32, 35, 45, 61, 77
JOHN DAVID PITTMAN

Interior photographs pages
22, 23, 31, 42, 81, 95
CHASEY HUDSON

———————————

Chief Executive Officer
CAROLINE KILMER

President
ART JOINNIDES

Chairman
JAY STEIN

Library of Congress Cataloging-in-Publication Data
available upon request.

ISBN: 978-1-68462-060-9

1 3 5 7 9 10 8 6 4 2

First Edition

Printed in China

I'd like to dedicate this book to all the kids out there with big hearts. Don't let the world change you. You change the world.

Contents

INTRODUCTION

YOU PROBABLY wouldn't call me your average fourteen-year-old. In some ways I guess I am. Candy is my favorite food. In another way, though, I am not so typical. It so happens that my favorite people in the world are nursing home seniors . . . and kindness is my hobby.

I am Ruby Chitsey, the founder and CEO of the nonprofit Three Wishes for Ruby's Residents. My advocacy for nursing home seniors has been featured in the news around the world. I've been on *Good Morning America,* CNN, *Fox News,* and the BBC! I was also a finalist for *Time* magazine's Kid of the Year. How cool is that? Just think that all this great stuff happened because I chose to be kind to others. A lot of people ask me why kindness is my hobby. It is actually my superpower, so let me explain a bit more.

MY
JOURNAL OF
WISHES.

KINDNESS BECAME MY HOBBY for three reasons. First, I'm pretty sure I was born that way. I was the kid to save every worm on the sunny concrete after a rainy day and I would save every tadpole I found in a mud puddle that was drying up. I didn't just see something that needed help, I took action. I feel like there has always been something deep inside me that made me want to help anything or anyone who needed it.

I think it's important to point out that I didn't just *want* to help. I did help. I took action. If anything made me different, it was that I did something to change the things I saw.

I remember when I received my first cellphone, I was so proud that I had my very own phone and number. I also saw it as an opportunity. I dropped little pieces of paper on the ground for people to find when we went out to town or the store. I didn't tell my parents I was doing this (they eventually found out). The notes I dropped said, "My name is Ruby Chitsey and I am ten years old. I want to make the life you live change." I drew a smiley face and I put my phone number on the back! I know now that this was not the brightest idea, but I was young and just wanted to help people.

At the time, I thought giving out my number to strangers was a genius plan, and I came up with it all on my own. I had seen people experiencing homelessness and I had done some volunteer work at a soup kitchen. I was learning that there were people out there who were going without and I wanted to make it better. This was one of my first real projects to change the world. It didn't work out so great, but that's okay, I was just getting started.

The second reason kindness became my hobby is because I was not like the other kids I knew. I tried the types of hobbies and activities that seemed to make my classmates really happy. You know, things like sports, dance, and cheer. I even tried a few art classes and running with my dad around the track. I didn't like any of them! Making a basket or running a fast 100-yard dash didn't seem to have the same kind of effect on me that it had on other kids.

Not liking the same activities as other kids made me feel as if something was wrong with me. But I found a way to solve that! I remember my mom dragging me to dance class in a leotard and those awful pink, itchy tights. I told her plain as day, "Mom, I don't like this. I just want to go with you to the nursing home. I am so much happier there." I think that was the day she actually saw it, too. She looked at me like I was crazy and she was suspicious. I'm not sure she believed me 100 percent, but I could tell something inside her had clicked. She probably just thought I was trying to get out of dance, and I was, but I meant it. I finished the short dance season and we agreed that I would spend more of my free time at the nursing home. She believed in me and she gave me a chance to prove to her that nursing home seniors could be my after-school activity and my hobby. I didn't disappoint her.

The final reason kindness became my hobby is because something made me see that kindness was a superpower that I didn't know I had. No one is perfect, right? I was born with a skin condition called keratosis pilaris. Let's just call it "KP." KP is caused because my skin makes too much protein and it creates bumps. KP is actually pretty common and I bet you know someone who has it and doesn't even know it. That is because KP usually shows up in the places of the body that you don't see, like the legs or the back of the arms. I was not as lucky as some people because my KP was only on my face. My skin condition was the first thing people usually saw and there were days I had hundreds of bumps on my face.

The sad part of this story is that I was bullied because of my skin condition. I was called ugly names at school and that hurt so badly. There were only a few kids who were mean to me, but there were a lot more who didn't stand up for me while I was being humiliated and that hurt worse. My mom noticed how much this bullying hurt me. My grades dropped twenty points and she said I quit smiling. She tried her best to cheer me up. We would go get ice cream after school and once she bought me a life-sized cardboard cutout of Justin Bieber!! My dad would give me the biggest hugs and even my brothers tried their best to make up for the meanness at school. My family did what they could to pick me up, but I will say it didn't cure the sadness I felt from being bullied. That was all about to change, though, and that is when the story gets even better!

One day, my classmates were the meanest they had ever been to me and I was at my lowest. I confided to my mom about how horrible my day was. She took me to McDonald's right after school. We drove straight there and she looked like she was on a serious mission of some sort. We didn't order anything for ourselves! Instead, she ordered about ninety orders of french fries. We live in a very small town and the McDonald's

Seniors are fun to be around.

employees probably thought we had lost our minds. They even asked my mom for her ID!!

We loaded the car with fries and raced up to a nursing home nearby so the fries would still be fresh. My mom told me it was my job to hand out the fries to my nursing home friends. Mom sat back and watched as I handed these fries to every senior I saw. It was magical. They transformed in front of me. I still remember their smiles. I don't think I had ever seen such happiness in my life. I was shocked that I did something to create such change in another human being. The staff even started crying. One of their grumpiest residents smiled for

the first time ever when he ate the first french fry. The staff couldn't believe the change in him. I changed so many people's lives that day with kindness and a dollar.

With my own eyes, I saw how an act of kindness changes people's lives. Most important of all, I felt it deep inside me. I felt like a million dollars. I felt invincible. I, Ruby Kate, had the power to change the world. I can't explain it, but being kind to the nursing home residents completely neutralized the meanness that had been thrown my way at school. It was almost like I had stumbled onto the cure and life for me was never going to be the same again. Kindness was a superpower for me and, from that day on, kindness was no doubt my hobby, my strength. It all made sense to me. I soared from helping others.

FOR AS LONG AS I CAN REMEMBER, I have spent a big chunk of my summers, after-school hours, and holidays at work with my mom. I was afraid of wheelchairs for a short time. That doesn't work out so well inside a nursing home where there are dozens of them. I got over that fear pretty quickly and before too long the facility would let me push some of the nursing home residents in their wheelchairs. I would bring them snacks and some of them would take me to the garden where they had pet turtles! Miss Fran taught me that a turtle's favorite food was a super-ripe banana. She was so sweet and I loved how much she knew about nature and animals. We would sneak inside the snack room and she would find us the brownest banana of all. Then we would walk a very short way to the garden courtyard and place pieces of banana on the ground. She taught me to wait quietly and patiently and, sure enough, within ten minutes a dozen turtles would come out of the garden and start eating the banana like madness! I was probably five years old then.

My great-grandmother, GiGi, also lived in a nursing home and I loved to visit her. She was the happiest when I brought her Cheetos. I taught her and her friends how to use a smart TV so they could watch old episodes of *The Bob Hope Show*. She was the only resident with a smart TV at that time and she had the most popular room around because of it! GiGi also loved to feed the facility dog, Russell. Russell was a senior, too. I don't know why, but GiGi was always convinced that Russell was starving (he was NOT), so GiGi split all of her meals with him. It was one of the best parts of her day when Russell came in for half her meal!

I also remember spending holidays like Halloween at the nursing home. They loved to see kids dressed up in their costumes and I would help them open their candy. It didn't feel like work to me. The nursing home was my playground. I loved it and I loved the seniors. I liked their hugs and I especially liked the way they made me feel. It was like they gave out "inside happiness" and I needed that. Many of them became my best friends. I even had a few of my birthday parties at the nursing home!

Before I go too much further, I want you to know that nursing home residents are just like us. They really are little versions of you and me but they are just

Here I am sitting with (from left to right) my kid brother Oliver, and biggest helpers, Sawyer and Leo.

seventy or eighty years older! Sometimes my friends come with me inside a nursing home and I can tell right away that they are intimidated and a little scared. I promise you don't have anything to be afraid of. I would bet that the people you meet inside the nursing home are going to be some of the nicest people you have ever met. You know what else? They are going to listen to every word you say. You know how sometimes our parents and siblings are too busy to hear about the coolest thing that happened today? That won't happen inside a nursing home. They are all ears and it feels great to talk to someone for that long and to know they've loved everything that was

said. So be fearless inside the nursing home and know you are about to meet some BFFs.

OK, back to how my project came about. When I was ten, I met a nursing home resident named Pearl who was watching her dog leave and she didn't know if she would see her ever again. I didn't know it, but Pearl was going to change my life. I used some of the money in my piggy bank to buy something to cheer up Pearl. And this is how my story of kindness began.

When I decided to help one nursing home senior, I learned that most nursing home seniors in America receive a very low "personal spending allowance" (PSA) each month that must cover everything from haircuts and clothes to pet food. My friends, like Pearl, in the nursing home were going without. I asked them, "What are your three wishes?" and all they wanted were simple things like fresh strawberries, pants that fit, and real cheese! If you asked kids my age that question you would get "a million dollars, AirPods, or a PlayStation." These seniors just wanted what most of us already have.

He wished for a Happy Meal. Little wishes, big impact.

My parents helped me fund the first three months of my project of fulfilling wishes. We shopped often and returned with the little things they needed. Their smiles and reactions to receiving something as simple as a cheese or fruit was my favorite part of the project. It was like I was handing out a million dollars.

My project kept growing and I began to fulfill wishes in other counties and cities. I decided to ask my parents for help to launch a fundraiser on a platform called GoFundMe. GoFundMe is a place on the web where you can share your project with the world and ask them for help funding it. So that's exactly what I did. I gathered the best photos of my project to use on my GoFundMe fundraiser. I also asked for help drafting the perfect description of what "Three Wishes" was.

I worked on my campaign for about four to five months before I published my project on GoFundMe in November of 2019 and I thought I might raise $1,000. I wasn't confident that normal people would find nursing home seniors interesting or be moved to help them through my project. It didn't stop me. I had hopes for success, but I really didn't expect it. I was totally wrong about America's reaction to my little nursing home project. Representatives from

GoFundMe called me within two weeks of publishing my story on their platform. They asked me to be one of their "Kid Heroes" and offered to share my project on a national scale. It was the happiest day of my life. They sent photographers to my hometown and assigned me to a team of amazing people to help me share my story. I felt like a queen with magical powers. I cried happy tears. I loved that someone else believed in my project and, most of all, I loved that I would be able to help the seniors more than ever. It was epic.

I am most proud and grateful that the people at GoFundMe took me seriously. I was ten years old and I had become used to hearing things like "you are too young" or "you can't accomplish that" or "you are just a little girl." GoFundMe employees believed in my project and gave me a giant way to share my story with the world. The rest is history.

My story was published nationally and I was contacted by people from across the entire world. I was featured in newspapers from India to Argentina. I gave 112 interviews in six months and people heard me loud and clear. They wanted to help. They wanted to know more.

Fast-forward to 2022 and I've founded the youth-led nonprofit Three Wishes for Ruby's Residents, which fulfills small wishes for nursing home seniors across America. Our nonprofit has fulfilled over 25,000 wishes from coast to coast.

Guess what? I also finally received a medal! I was so happy the day I received my first-ever award and medal. I thought you could only get an award for shooting the most baskets or being the fastest at something. But I received awards for being kind to seniors. If you took a quick tour of my room, you would think I was a star athlete because I have awards and medals from wall to wall and on every shelf. I had a flag flown in my honor by the U.S. Air Force in Afghanistan. To date, I've received the highest honors a youth can receive for my humanitarian work. My hometown declared March 19 as Ruby Kate Chitsey Day and I was the first person to ever receive the keys to the city of Harrison! But please don't misunderstand me. I didn't do this for the medals. I did this because I loved it, but it does feel great to be recognized by people, friends, and even strangers. My favorite thing is that I've taught kids and adults from all over the country how to help nursing home seniors in their communities.

We are changing their world. It's a movement.

1

Kindness Toward Seniors Starts with You

Start Visiting Seniors and Granting Wishes in Your Community

IT'S IMPORTANT TO DECIDE HOW YOU WANT TO HELP seniors before you get started. In my opinion, volunteer work is more fun when you help in ways that make you happy.

I love to do the "three wishes project" with seniors because I love their reactions. I love to see them smile when I hand them a candy bar or a pair of shoes. Their reaction makes me feel like I won a million dollars.

My brother loves to read. So he likes to help seniors by collecting great books for them. My friend Leo absolutely loves cats and LEGOs, so he prefers to help seniors by collecting LEGOs and pet food for them. Another one of our kid board members, Sawyer, is an amazing singer, cook, and party planner. He likes to help nursing home seniors by singing in their facilities, planning huge parties and luaus, and even performing skits for the residents. Arsh is an artist in Iowa. He helps seniors by teaching them how to paint and create art! All of my friends found a way to connect with seniors by doing something they already loved!

What do you like to do, and can you use that to help seniors? Nursing homes have lots of needs, so it's not too hard to find a good way to help them!

In this book, I will introduce ways that you can help seniors in your community. We will talk about donating hygiene kits, planning book and pet food drives, fulfilling small wishes, and sending good old snail mail! Think about which of these types of projects you want to help with first. Then you can move on to finding a facility that needs your help.

FIND SENIORS IN YOUR COMMUNITY

Remember, we are looking for seniors who live in a long-term care facility of some kind. This includes retirement centers, assisted living, skilled nursing facilities, traditional nursing homes, and low-income senior apartments. These places come in all shapes and sizes. I have seen facilities with as few as twenty-six seniors living in them to as large as 380!!! Facilities also house seniors of every type. Some might be rich, others poor, some might be lonely, and others may have tons of family and support.

I suggest getting an adult to help you do a web search for "long-term care facilities near me." In my area, more than fifteen facilities will pop up on my search screen. Print a list of facilities and ask an adult to do a "drive-by" to check them out from the outside. You can't judge a book by its cover, but when I am looking for a new facility, I will usually start with the ones that look a little older on the outside. Older, less modern facilities in my area are more likely to need and accept my help. This won't always be true, but it helps speed things up sometimes.

If you pick a facility that looks more like a Ritz-Carlton hotel, you will have to make sure to offer to help their seniors in ways that would suit their needs. They might not need snacks, hygiene kits, and sodas but might love your art, postcards, and visits.

I also try to take note of the size of the facilities I see. If I am looking to sponsor a gigantic project, I will make sure to identify facilities that are very big. If I am looking to sponsor a smaller project, I try to stick with the facilities that are smaller in size. The first step is to start making some phone calls. There is no magic in picking the right facility to call first, just pick one and work your way down the list.

Make a checklist that includes the following and have it ready when you make the call:

- Get the name of the facility.

- Call the facility and ask for their social director or marketer.

- Have your "speech" written out and know exactly what you are offering (do you want to do the Three Wishes Project, donate books or hygiene kits, etc.). Here are some examples of what you can say to the nursing home, depending on which type of project you have chosen:

"Hello. My name is _____ and I am _____ years old. I would like to know if any of your residents have any small needs. I would like to do the Three Wishes Project at your facility. It is a free service project. I'd like to ask some of your residents if they have three small wishes. Some common wishes are a favorite candy bar, book, T-shirt, soda, or activity like a set of cards or a puzzle. Could I arrange a time to come to your facility and interview residents? I would make a list of their needs and return in a week or so to hand them out to them."

Who doesn't love chocolate?

If the facility is not allowing visits, here are a few other ways to do the project:

● *"Could you ask your residents if they have one to three small needs? I could pick up the list from you and return with the items in _____ days or weeks"*

● *"I would like to come to sing at your facility. Is there a good day for my group to do that?"*

● *"I would like to update your library with great books. Is that something your residents could use?"*

If they say they have a need, go to the next step. If they say they can't use your help, ask them to suggest a facility nearby that might have residents who would benefit from this project and just try again. I have made five phone calls before finding the right facility that needs my help. Be persistent and know that you will find a facility.

● Ask for the name of your contact person and the best way to reach them (phone, email, etc.).

● If you arrange a time to interview residents, ask how many residents will be participating. You need to know if it's twenty or a hundred.

GET INVOLVED AND RECEIVE DONATIONS FOR YOUR PROJECT

We have talked about how to choose a project and how to find a facility; now let's discuss how to fund your project and get some friends to help you carry it out.

Ask yourself these questions before asking others to help you with your project:

- How big do you want your first project to be? A project involving 300 seniors will mean that you will need lots of help from friends and family, but a project involving thirty residents can probably be completed with just a few people.

- What is your budget? How much money are you willing to spend or how many items do you think you could collect?

- Where will you collect the wish items? People who are donating will need a mailing address or drop-off point.

It's important to talk about small wishes and what that means. It shouldn't cost a lot of money to fulfill small wishes. Remember the photo of my friend with the Happy Meal? That act of kindness costs four dollars. It's amazing what a big impact a small wish can have.

Here is a true story about what I did with a three-dollar donation that might give you some great ideas of how far you can stretch a dollar.

Our nonprofit has a community center on the historic square in Harrison, Arkansas. It is a large space that is open to the public. It is a place where the young and the old connect, do crafts, and share stories.

Lots of people walk in off the street to check out our community center or make a donation. One day a man walked in. He might have been a zillionaire but I don't think so. He wanted to know what our place was and what our purpose was. We told him that we fulfill small wishes for nursing home seniors. He reached down

This is the headquarters for my nonprofit.

and pulled out his wallet (it didn't have much in it) and he gave us three dollars. I could tell this meant a lot to him and it meant a lot to me, too.

This is what I did with that three dollars: I bought three of my nursing home friends some of their most favorite things.

I bought Bea a Little Debbie strawberry roll because that is her favorite thing in the world.

I bought Mary R two bananas because she's crazy about bananas. She's a

diabetic and it's hard for her to have fresh fruit. Her smile when I give her a banana is the best.

Lastly, I bought a small package of cat treats for Steve because he LOVES cats and he wants the facility cat, Sweetie, to come sleep in his bed so badly. These treats will make that happen.

I have no idea what the man's name was who donated the three dollars. I don't know his story, but you can see that I made sure his three dollars mattered BIG.

Keep this story in mind as you ask your community for help with your project. I suggest starting your fundraiser by writing out a short, clear description of your project. For example:

"My name is _____ and I am _____ years old. I am fulfilling small wishes (donating books, collecting hygiene products, art, etc.) for _____ [put the number of residents you are helping here] nursing home seniors in our community. You can help me by making a cash donation, signing up to volunteer, or dropping off any of the following wish items to this address _____."

IMPORTANT DO'S AND DON'TS WHEN ASKING FOR HELP

- Do not use the name of the resident or facility you have chosen to help when spreading the word about your project. Some facilities do not want the public to know they've accepted help and many seniors are embarrassed to accept help.

Something as simple as "I am helping a local nursing facility" is all you should need to say to ask for donations and help.

- Accept money or goods. Many people are more likely to donate a product (book, food, shampoo) than money. Either type of donation will help make your project a big success!

Once you have written a short description of your project you will need to choose how you want to spread the word, gather support, and get donations.

Here are some great ways to get the help you need:

- SOCIAL MEDIA: Attach the description of your project along with some photos of kids fulfilling wishes for seniors. A picture says a thousand words. You can find free photos of the Three Wishes Project on our nonprofit's website or our Facebook page. A great photo will motivate people to help.

- FLYERS: Type something up and ask local principals for permission to give the flyer to their students. Post your flyer in public spaces.

Dear Principal

I would like to ask for your permission to post a flyer at our school. I have found out that local nursing home seniors need our help. I would like to ask students to help me collect books, toiletries, unwanted art, handwritten letters and small snack items for the seniors. I have attached an example of my flyer. You can reach me at any of the contacts below.

☏ +123-456-7890
⦿ 123 Anywhere St., Any City
✉ youremail@gmail.com

I've used letters and flyers just like these to help gain support for projects.

- **SPORTS CLUBS:** Reach out to your local volleyball, soccer, etc., teams and tell them about your project. Quite often these teams will ask their players to collect goods on your behalf. You might be surprised to find out just how many snacks a sports team can collect! The team just might fulfill half of your needs!

- **CHURCHES:** Ask local churches if they will put your project in their weekly newsletter and be sure to list specific wish items that their members can donate.

- **CLUBS:** This includes groups like the Boy Scouts, Girl Scouts, homeschooling groups, and Future Farmers of America (FFA). They may also lend a hand in collecting goods for your project if you ask them.

- **REAL ESTATE AGENCIES:** This is one of the best types of businesses to seek out for help for your project. Ask them to help you make a challenge to other real estate companies to see who can get the most wish items donated. This is a fun and very successful way to obtain the wish items you need and it can work great with those really big facilities, too.

GIVE KINDNESS, IT'S FREE

When I think of the word "kindness," I think of little things I can do to make another person feel better. I consider it as giving away "inside happiness." And kindness is free. It doesn't cost a thing to make a senior smile. It also doesn't have to be hard or complicated. I'm always on the lookout for how to help in small ways. That means that I'm paying attention when I'm out and about and especially when I am anywhere that I might see seniors.

What are some ways you can give kindness for free?

Here is a list of some of my favorite projects that I will explain more about a little later in the book.

- Smile at seniors as you go about your day. Make eye contact and give them a compliment. This simple act of kindness lets them know you saw them and you noticed they are a part of our world.

- Small acts: Open the door. Give them your seat. Help them reach an item in the store.

- Mail them a letter that just says I hope you have a great day.

Connecting During a Pandemic

The COVID-19 pandemic has kept people like me from going inside nursing homes at different times, so we have learned to connect with the essential staff who care for the nursing home residents. We call nursing homes and ask for the email address of the person in charge of activities. We work alongside staff like this to get a list of wishes anytime we aren't allowed at the bedside!

I can't explain it, but for some reason their candy bars taste so much better when they come in a bag decorated with art from a kindergartner!

- Paint a kindness rock for their garden.

- Interview them! I love to ask questions about what it was like living in the 1920s. Many of our seniors didn't have modern plumbing or refrigerators!

- Offer to refill the bird feeders at a local nursing home.

- Offer to plant a garden at a local nursing home.

- Donate great books to a nursing home.

- Send a stack of anonymous postcards with kind messages to a nursing facility.

- Offer to donate pet food to residents who might be struggling to feed their pets.

- Try to find a senior pen pal.

- Donate some good shampoo, soaps, and lotions.

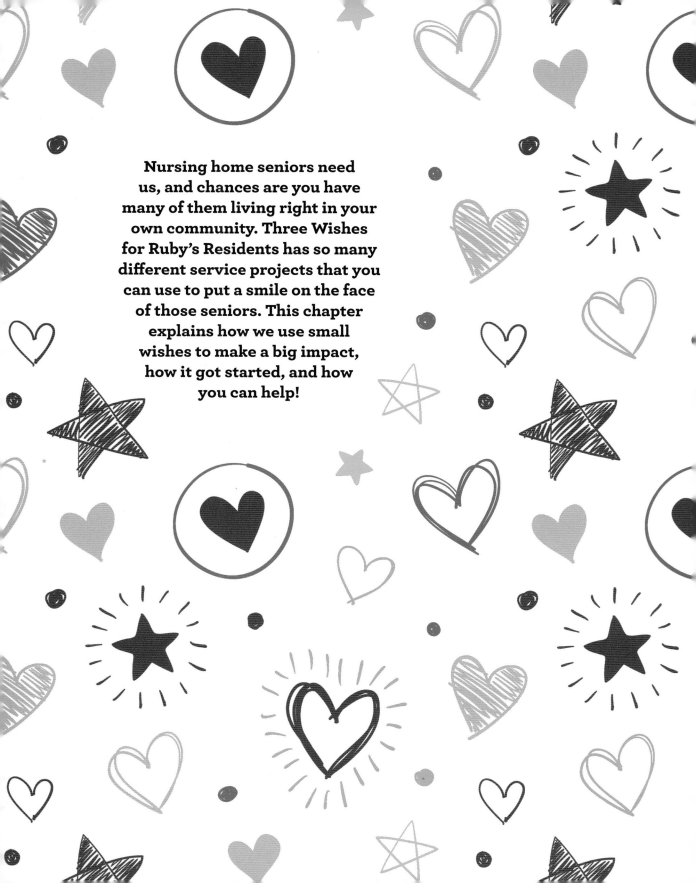

Nursing home seniors need us, and chances are you have many of them living right in your own community. Three Wishes for Ruby's Residents has so many different service projects that you can use to put a smile on the face of those seniors. This chapter explains how we use small wishes to make a big impact, how it got started, and how you can help!

2

The Projects for Ruby's Residents

Three Wishes Project

> "No act of kindness, no matter how small, is ever wasted"
>
> –Aesop

THIS IS A FUN PROJECT that fulfills small wishes for nursing home seniors. It is my favorite project because I love to see the reactions of the seniors when they receive their wishes. The Three Wishes Project can be done by you or by nursing home staff, depending on visitation rules. The first step is to interview nursing home residents and find out what little wishes or needs they have. If you are allowed inside the facility, you could do this yourself. If not, you will need to ask your nursing home contact person to obtain the wish list for you.

The wishes could be something as simple as their favorite candy bar, a takeout meal, or a new pair of shoes. They will probably need you to give them some examples of what a "wish" is. Make a list and fulfill the wishes! This isn't just about the residents who are low on money. Some residents are just low on family or maybe they don't have a way to get to the store. There are lots of reasons that nursing home seniors may need their favorite snack. It doesn't matter to me why they need it. If it will make them smile, I'll do my best to get it for them.

Not every resident will have a wish and some might only have one or two wishes. It's surprising for me to hear the wishes the nursing home seniors request because they can be so small. I mean, who wishes for something like shampoo, right? I know if I asked kids my age what their three wishes were, they would list big things like iPads, money, smartphones, and designer sneakers. But that is not what I usually hear from a nursing home senior. When I ask them what they need, it's usually something that most people already have plenty of. Some of the most common wishes are soda, shampoo, and a favorite snack.

It's rare, but every now and then a senior will have a wish that I can't fulfill.

MY WISH?

LIPSTICK

All she wanted was lipstick.

I remember one day a senior asked me to provide satellite cable for the entire nursing home. I really wanted to do that for her, but the reality is that I could not fulfill that wish. I told her to talk to the owners of the nursing home about satellite TV and then I helped her find a channel so that she could watch her favorite baseball team. I found a way to make her smile, but it was not by fulfilling the wish she asked for. So my best advice to you if this happens is to be honest and tell them that it isn't something you can do and try to offer a substitute that makes them happy.

I'll never forget the first time I asked seniors for their three wishes. Part of me expected them to ask for vacations, money, and Lamborghinis, but another part of me knew that they would not. I had seen their bare rooms and walls. I had not seen people come to visit them. It didn't shock me when the first man only asked for pants that fit. The others simply asked me for warm jackets, fresh fruit, and something as simple as a six-pack of their favorite soda. Some of the more unusual wishes included prayer, a hug, and a ticket to a water park.

One of my favorite residents, Myrtle, always asks me for a candy called circus peanuts, and that only costs one dollar! Her face lights up when I give her this candy and her smile makes me feel I can do anything.

Sweet Henrietta (aka The Cat Lady) would ask me for cat food plus she shared garden secrets and homemade goodies with me, too! Henrietta introduced me to zucchini bread, which is shockingly delicious despite the icky name. She also taught me that a lady should never be seen without a little lipstick. Henrietta was naturally beautiful and she was right about the lipstick. It made her even more beautiful. Christine usually asks for fresh "cuties," those small tangerines. It's so easy to fulfill their wishes. Anyone can do it.

Myrtle and me with the circus peanuts. That smile is my favorite part about the Three Wishes Project.

HOW DID THE THREE WISHES PROJECT GET STARTED?

PEARL & RUBY

One day at the nursing home with my mom, I noticed a lady staring out the window for way too long. I thought maybe she saw something fun outside like a baby bird or an ambulance. I asked the lady what she was staring at for so long. I learned that her name was Pearl and she told me she was watching her dog leave the nursing home for the last time. Pearl had just given up her dog, GiGi (same name as my great-grandmother), and she was sad. GiGi was one of those "hotdog" dogs, a dachshund, and she was Pearl's best friend for eleven years.

Pearl and I became instant BFFs because we are both named after a jewel and we had both just lost a pet we adored. My dog Ziggy disappeared without a trace and I was still very sad about that.

I found out that Pearl only received forty dollars a month from the government to take care of herself and her dog. She skipped haircuts and went without the "little things" for a long time to save money to take care of GiGi, but on the day I met her, she had just given GiGi away forever. Pearl just didn't have enough money to take care

of herself and her dog.

My encounter with Pearl that day is what led me to start the Three Wishes Project. I found out that most nursing home seniors were living off a very small allowance. In Arkansas, that allowance is forty dollars and it has been that amount since 1999. The stipend in North Carolina is thirty dollars. I knew I had to do something.

The first thing I did was try to cheer up Pearl. I gave her some pizza she wanted. Then, I decided to ask all the residents, "If I could grant you three small wishes, what would they be?" Pearl didn't want much and that surprised me.

She asked for the pizza, a pet to love, and a teddy bear. I had the sweetest man ask me for a McDonald's Happy Meal. Ronnie, another nursing home resident, just wanted pants that fit. I thought to myself, "I can do this. I can buy all of these things at our local superstore." I made a list of their wishes and my parents took me to a store to purchase them. I returned to the nursing home and I gave the residents the little things they asked for.

Since it started, the Three Wishes Project has received a phenomenal amount of support from the community for collecting wish items. Many beauty pageant contestants will host a snack drive for us and we can collect hundreds of snacks for seniors this way. Local veterinarians and regular citizens donate pet food. We have fresh fruit and veggie drives in the summer and people will drop off garden items all summer. We have sweet ladies who make handmade quilts. Our local Walmart donated all the unsold Mother's Day flowers one year. McDonald's gives us a discount so we can buy seniors Happy Meals often. It's their most requested fast food meal. We accept books and old iPhones, iPads, and Kindles all year. We receive hundreds of wish items from our community every month. We also speak every chance we get at places like the Lions Club, Rotary, schools, and church groups to let them know what we need and how they can help.

My absolute favorite part about granting the wishes was the residents' reactions. Some residents cried happy tears and others had the most genuine smiles I'd ever seen. Who ever thought that a Happy Meal would make someone cry? I didn't. They hugged me tight and I could tell in those moments that I had really changed a life. I could change the world one step at a time.

The nursing home residents taught me what it truly means to be grateful. I had no idea that so many people in my community were going without something as simple as fresh fruit and good pants.

There is barely a day or two that goes by when someone local doesn't come up to me and thank me for what I do with the Three Wishes Project. I've been called an angel on earth, one of a kind, inspiring, America's granddaughter. The families of seniors thank me every chance they get for brightening the life of their parents or for just making them smile. But most of my nursing home friends don't have family. Really, I am the only family or visitor they have. With the Three Wishes Project, I get

HUGS ARE FREE.

What about the other half? What about the ones who don't receive a small stipend? Well, we help them, too. Everyone could use a little kindness and some extra attention. We make sure ALL nursing home seniors feel the love regardless of their income.

I admit that one of my favorite things to do is find nursing homes that need us the most. I bet you have some nursing home seniors who could use your help right inside your community. They could be skipping haircuts and trying to figure out how to pay their cellphone bills or maybe they just haven't had a visitor in a long time. What is really sad is that way too often they are simply just going without. You can help them!

As of writing this book, we fulfill about 1,000 wishes a month and in a big month like December we can fulfill 5,000 to 10,000. We have about 250 wishes a week and we deliver those every Tuesday and Friday, and a few dozen or so on the weekends. We deliver the wishes within a few days or a week at the most.

to step in as family and a friend. Now everyone has a reason to smile.

PROBLEM SOLVED!

The Three Wishes Project is the best remedy for the nursing home blues. It makes nursing home seniors feel loved and it provides them with the small things that make life sweet. Who wants to spend the rest of their days without their favorite soda or candy bar? Not me. We have 1.4 million nursing home seniors in the United States. More than half receive a small government check.

YOU CAN DO IT, TOO!

Here's how you can do the Three Wishes Project. Do some research and find a "long-term care facility" near you. "Long-term care facility" is just a fancy word for any facility that houses senior citizens on a long-term basis. These could be senior apartment complexes, assisted living facilities, retirement centers, skilled nursing facilities, and traditional nursing homes.

Reach out to any of these long-term care facilities in your area by calling or emailing the activity director. The most important question to ask them is whether or not they have residents living in their facility who need your help. Not every nursing home will have residents who need or want our help.

It's important to make sure you connect with a facility that houses residents who need small wishes fulfilled. Once you have found a facility, just tell the activity director you want to do the Three Wishes Project for some or all of their residents. This is a great time to exchange email addresses so you can send a note describing the Three Wishes Project in more detail. What is the "Three Wishes Project"? It's a youth-led project that seeks to fulfill small needs or wishes for anyone living in a long-term care center. That's the short answer!

Ask the activity director to find three small things that the residents need. Be sure to give them some examples of common wishes, like chocolate bars, pants, shoes, or a favorite snack. This will give them a guide to have as they ask the residents for small needs and it will keep you from getting wishes like a giant HDTV set!! The focus is on "small."

Leave a contact phone number or email so the activity director can send a completed wish list to you. Share the completed wish list on social media, at school, or host a fundraiser to fulfill the wishes. Ask local elementary school teachers to help you write letters and create art to include with the wishes. I can't explain it, but for some reason their candy bars taste so much better when they come with a little piece of art from a kindergartner.

Once the wish list is fulfilled, contact the facility again to simply drop off the wishes. There is a chance you will not be able to deliver the wishes yourself, so be sure to ask about visitation policies. Be sure to take photos of your project before, during, and after and ask the facility if they could take and share photos of the residents' reactions to the wishes. Finally, share your success and project to spark others to fulfill wishes for seniors across America.

WE MAKE A DIFFERENCE!

Most people think of a hobby as something like basketball, art, cheer, or robotics. My friend Ava Grayce is an artist. My older brother is a baseball player. In fact, both of my brothers are very fast. They can win the 50-yard dash every time, but not me. I never won an award for anything until I started volunteering. I know what it feels like to be the kid who never gets a medal and who finishes last. It can make you feel left out and like you are not good enough. I found out that I was really good at helping others. I discovered that volunteer work could be my hobby just like baseball was my brother's hobby. I also found out that you can get medals for being kind. I received my first ever award in 2019, and many others since then, including the highest honor a youth can get for volunteer services. Now my wall is pretty full of medals, trophies, and awards.

The Three Wishes Project is a great way to see if you like being a volunteer. There are probably plenty of seniors around you who could use the help, and the project will make you smile, too.

Here I am delivering wishes. The rolling cart is a great way to make deliveries inside a nursing home.

I love to volunteer with nursing home seniors. I love their stories and perfect smiles. I love the way they light up when they see one of us. I think they are the greatest people on the planet. Not many people choose to help them, but we can change that through the Three Wishes Project.

Mobile Book Cart for Seniors

"The more you read, the more things you will know. The more that you learn, the more places you will go."

–Dr. Seuss

How do nursing home seniors usually stay busy? Well, many of them read. Senior citizens are voracious readers. They have been reading all of their lives. Printed materials keep them busy, connected, and up-to-date on current events. I know residents who will spend half their morning devouring the local newspaper. So we want to make sure that nursing home seniors have easy access to a great selection of high-quality books and materials like magazines and newspapers. This section will explain how we keep nursing homes stocked with the books seniors love.

Many people don't know what to do with their books after they read them. Give them a reason to recycle the book to a nursing home senior by hosting a book drive!

Many nursing home seniors don't have the same hobbies as you and I. They rarely watch TV shows anymore and they don't play video games, or even get to leave the nursing home very often. The other day I was having lunch with a ninety-year-old and she had never heard of YouTube. It is not that they are behind the times, they just like to read print whereas most of us are more used to digital media.

There are 1.4 million seniors in America's nursing homes. Most of these facilities have small libraries, but they are not always updated.

The mobile book cart program was created after I discovered that many of the seniors I knew in nursing homes had poor access to good books. Their library was stocked with thrift store castoffs and low-quality books that most people would not enjoy reading. My brother also found out that approximately 320 million books are discarded each year in America. That's a lot of books in our landfills in just one year! I have found that nursing home seniors can't afford a new book or newspaper subscription, can't get a ride to the local library, or simply have a library stocked with not-so-good books. That's a shame because it is so easy to recycle a good book and plenty of people have a great book or two to donate.

Throughout the year we host a used book drive. We ask people to donate their new or used books to us! Through email and social media, I get the word out to fellow readers that I want their used books for my senior residents. I store the books at my nonprofit organization and deliver a cart of books to nursing home facilities each month. The mobile book cart is packed with books seniors will enjoy. It's basically a library on wheels. We also include audiobooks, magazines, newspapers, musical CDs, and some fun activities like crossword puzzles, coloring books, and markers.

HOW DID THE MOBILE BOOK CART GET STARTED?

I appreciate a good book. My parents make sure I read every day, but I don't like reading a book that I didn't choose. If you told me to read a big book about the history of corn, I am not sure I could get through it and I'm pretty sure I wouldn't enjoy it.

My brother likes to read fantasy books, but his school library doesn't have a big selection of those types of books. He knows exactly what it feels like to want to read a certain type of book but have little access to it. At least my brother can ask our parents to take him to the local county library or even a big bookstore.

But what about nursing home seniors? They can't just hop in a car and get to a library. Many can't afford a brand-new book, especially not on their small monthly allowance. Buying a new book could be a third of all the money that they have to last them the month. Yikes! Yearly magazine subscriptions are quite

Wilma and Billy the Kid

Wilma is over a 100 years old and she is doing some research on Billy the Kid. She thinks there is a chance that her father encountered Billy the Kid in the 1870s. She loves it when we bring books that have anything to do with the Wild West and especially Billy the Kid. Wilma doesn't drive anymore, and she's outlived all her children. It's not easy for her to get to the library and she doesn't shop online! Our book cart is a lifesaver for people like her.

affordable but newspaper subscriptions can cost way over $125 a year and most simply can't afford that.

A lack of access to books is why they need our help. I met a lady named Zella at a nursing home and she reads a book every two days! She told me one of her favorite things was to get her hands on a new book and she even liked the smell of books! I had no idea someone could read as much as she does. She doesn't like TV, radio, music, games, or puzzles. She just likes to read.

But Zella also has old eyes. She needs the books in large print—these are books that have words that are bigger than usual. I was shocked to see the "library" in her nursing home was stocked with thrift store castoff books and books you and I would probably not enjoy reading. All the books came from donations. From what I could tell, people were donating junky books with missing covers and pages. I didn't see many great titles, audiobooks, large print, or even bestsellers.

I also had several nursing home seniors wish for a subscription to the daily newspaper. Most of these residents had a morning routine before they moved into a nursing home, which included spending several hours reading every inch of the daily newspaper. They

Seniors love to read books.

especially liked doing the crossword puzzle. Their routine was changed when they came to the nursing home and suddenly, for whatever reason, there were no newspapers to read. Now they have a huge chunk of time in their morning and they would love to have the newspaper back.

Zella inspired me to start a library for people like her. My brother Oliver came up with the idea of hosting a national book drive. He did some research about the number of books that end up in U.S. landfills and discovered that by recycling books for nursing home seniors, he would be helping to reduce waste. Oliver used social media resources like Facebook, Instagram, and YouTube, local churches and schools, local newspapers,

We like to use crates for the boxes of books. They are sturdy, easy to carry, and seniors can access the crates easily from wheelchairs.

and flyers and handouts to ask people from across America to mail us their unwanted but great books. It worked. We collected over 1,000 amazing books by the end of the first year.

PROBLEM SOLVED!

Each month our nursing home residents can check out a book from our cart and they can spend all the time they need to finish reading it. Once they've finished the book, they can either return it to our cart or exchange it with another nursing home resident.

We try to make sure we have what individual people like best. Zella loves thrillers and mysteries, but Bobby's crazy about westerns. Westerns are hard to find, but, with help from book donors, we somehow keep residents like Bobby supplied with a fresh western book every month.

Blind readers and the residents who can no longer hold a book in their hands are also in need of good books. Most states have an official "library for the blind" and we can get free audiobooks and audio readers for our residents through these types of organizations. An audiobook is a book that is read aloud. The audio reader is the device that plays the narrated book. Once a resident gets the audio reader device, they can check out as many audiobooks as they like through the libraries for the blind.

Marie is a nursing home resident who is blind from a stroke but loves to read. She asked us to help her find a way to read *Gone with the Wind*. She loves the story of Scarlett and Rhett Butler. We contacted the Arkansas Library for the Blind and they sent her a free copy of *Gone with the Wind* along with a very nice audio reader. She was so thrilled.

It's so hard for a blind senior citizen in a nursing home to find a source of entertainment. Audiobooks are truly a game changer for someone like Marie. The audiobooks keep her mind busy and help make long days seem much shorter.

YOU CAN DO IT, TOO!

Anyone can host a used book drive. Let your community know you're collecting books for nursing home seniors or seniors in any long-term care living center.

Mention how much seniors love to read and that you want to give them a better collection of books and keep the books out of your landfills. Spread the word through social media, flyers to schools and churches, the local newspaper, and by word of mouth. Let people know what you're looking for— good books in good shape, audiobooks, large print, etc. The most popular genres are westerns, historical fiction, and romance novels. We like to include new activity books such as crossword puzzles, word finds, and coloring books.

Set up boxes for book donations at local businesses or schools. Collect, sort, and label the books, especially if you only have a limited supply. The label is great for letting people know where the books came from and also for placing instructions on how to return them to you if needed. For example, at first, we put our nonprofit logo and "please return to" on our labels for the books. We were worried about not having enough books when we started, so the label helps people return books to us after they have read them.

Once you collect fifty or more books, I suggest sorting them by style or genre. Then simply drop an assortment of books off at your partnering nursing facility. The crate is also easy to drop at the door of the facility in case visitation is limited.

If you can, include personal touches and surprises in the books. You can make homemade bookmarks with kind messages, sweet cards, or a piece of student art to put inside the book.

This is a project you can do once a year or even each season to keep a fresh rotation of books.

Pet Meals on Wheels

> "You must be the change you wish to see in the world."
>
> -Mahatma Gandhi

SENIOR CITIZENS ARE just like us. Two things that I think about that we have in common are pets and food! Did you know that most people in America own a pet? It doesn't matter if you are young or old; the fact is that most people have pets!

We all love to eat, right? Nutritious meals are important, but do you ever stop to think about how your food gets to your house? Senior citizens can have trouble getting to the store, driving, and buying their food and pet food. This is not a new problem and it's why nearly every community in America has a program called Meals on Wheels. It's exactly what it says, a free service that delivers meals to senior citizens' homes.

COLLECTING
PET FOOD
FOR PET
MEALS ON
WHEELS

I found out that many of the seniors in the Meals on Wheels mobile food program were sharing their food with their pets. They would eat half their lunch and give the other half to their pet. That makes a lot of sense. If you are already struggling to feed yourself, I can totally see why you would also struggle to feed your pet. That is why our nonprofit started a program called Pet Meals on Wheels. We put pet food on the delivery trucks!

HOW DID PET MEALS ON WHEELS GET STARTED?

I started Pet Meals on Wheels because I saw a problem. I saw seniors on a limited income struggling to feed their pets and that made me sad. I wanted to find a way that I could help them. I love pets as much as I love people. I have three cats and three dogs. I have had a cat in my life since the day I was born. I don't know what it is like to live without a pet and it

hurts my heart to think there are seniors in my community whose pets are hungry.

I meet nursing home residents and seniors who have pets all the time. I met a nursing home resident named Lawrence. He had never lived without a cat. He told me that the day he moved into the nursing home was the first day in his life he lived without a cat. He was really funny because I asked him what his cat's name was. He told me he actually had "dozens of cats" and he always called them by their color. He said his favorite cat was called Yellow.

I understand why people like me have pets but I also really understand why senior citizens have pets. So many of them are not only lonely, but they live alone, too. Sometimes their pet is really their only BFF and may even be the only other "person" in their household. Their pets mean the whole world to them and they want to spoil them just like we do.

Seniors also love their pets like crazy. Have you ever heard someone say, "I love you so much I could gobble you up"? My grandmother used to say that all the time about me and I hear seniors say this about their pets. I love to cuddle with my cat Gilbert. He is a giant tabby cat. He is orange with a big, soft belly and it sounds like a little bitty motor when he purrs next to me. Gilbert also loves to eat. I couldn't stand it if I was unable to feed him when he was hungry, so I knew this was a problem that I wanted to solve and I knew I would need help from my community to do that.

I was already familiar with the Meals on Wheels program because I had volunteered at one before. Plus, Meals on Wheels is pretty common all across America. You may have even seen one of their trucks in your neighborhood delivering meals. In 2020, I was on a TV show and I traveled around the country volunteering with many

different types of organizations. When I was in Kentucky, I spent a week with some workers and volunteers from a big Meals on Wheels program. I think they served food to over 10,000 seniors! I paid attention during my week at their nonprofit because I saw so many ways that I could help similarly in my community.

One of the saddest things I ever saw was a senior who had run out of dry cat food. I noticed she had pieces of an oatmeal pie outside her sliding glass door. The oatmeal pie had obviously been pinched up carefully into bite-size pieces and tossed out onto the ground. I couldn't imagine why my senior friend Mary had done something so weird. She told me it was for her cats. She had completely run out of dry cat food and all she had to give them were oatmeal pies. Of course, the first thing I did was make sure she received some cat food, pronto! I also knew I never wanted to see this again in my life. I saw a problem and I wanted to fix it.

We were able to tour some of the seniors' homes who received the mobile meals in Kentucky and almost all of them had pets. When I returned to Arkansas, I continued my volunteer work inside the nursing homes. After the oatmeal pie tragedy and after meeting

Seniors don't want to worry about how they will feed their pets. Everyone is happier when their needs are met.

people like Lawrence, I started to ask seniors if they struggled at home to feed their pets. Way too many of them did. Turns out that Mary and Lawrence were just two of many seniors who needed help with their pets.

I decided to ask my community, friends, school, and local veterinarians for pet food donations. I just asked for dry cat and dog food and I explained that seniors struggle to feed themselves and their pets. I asked my friend Leo to help me get in touch with our local Meals

on Wheels program. We just googled their number and started making calls. It took lots of phone calls and we had to ask our parents to make some calls, too. We didn't give up. After a few months of planning, we were able to get a list of the number of seniors in the Meals on Wheels program who needed cat food or dog food or both.

We started with about twenty seniors who needed pet food. As word spread of our project, we began to get phone calls and messages from other seniors in the community who were struggling to feed their pets. We received calls from senior apartments, retirement centers, and local nursing home residents. Turns out pet food had become way out of their budget. Leo and I would count the number of seniors in need at the beginning of each month and our parents or volunteers would deliver pet food to the food trucks and to the many senior living centers that needed the food.

PROBLEM SOLVED!

My nonprofit and I have tackled the problem of senior citizens' pets being hungry in our community. It took a lot of us working together to solve the problem, but we did it! Teamwork is so important when you are trying to solve a problem. I couldn't have accomplished this by myself. I like to say, "No more hungry pets!" Do you think you have seniors who could use some help feeding their pets?

Let's talk about what happens as you get older. The pets don't just disappear, right? Many senior citizens have pets just like us. Some seniors are low on funds and others can't just jump in the car and go grab some pet food whenever they run out. Maybe they can't drive anymore, maybe their check hasn't

come in for the month, or maybe they had an unexpected water leak that cost them the money they usually have for pet food. A friend of mine once told me that availability doesn't guarantee accessibility. To put that more simply, just because there might be a lot of pet food at the store doesn't mean the seniors in your community have easy access to it.

YOU CAN DO IT, TOO!

I can think of a few ways you can help provide pet food to seniors in need. Chances are you have a Meals on Wheels program right in your own community. I suggest having an adult give them a call and see if they accept volunteers. Sometimes the best way to understand a program is to dive in and get some hands-on experience. That is what I did in Kentucky. Volunteering inside Meals on Wheels was a huge step for me. I learned so much about what it means to be uncertain about how you will get your next meal and how sad that is. I met seniors in the program face to face and I was able to appreciate their struggle even more (and see their pets!). I would give your local Meals on Wheels a call and ask if they could use your help in any way.

You can also look around your community for places that house seniors. Look for senior apartment complexes, assisted living centers, retirement centers, and nursing homes. Each of these places should have a manager or a person in charge who could tell you if they have any residents who could use some help with feeding their pets. Many communities also have an Area Agency on Aging. This is a great resource for finding seniors who need help. The Area Agency on Aging often operates senior centers. They might be able to help you find seniors who need some help or even let you create a pet food pantry at one of their centers. Remember, it doesn't matter if you help one senior or a hundred

seniors. What matters is that you do something to help. That's the best place to start.

The easiest part is collecting the pet food. You can post flyers or make social media posts about a pet food drive. Make sure you have arranged a place for people to drop off the donated pet food. Pass the information about the pet food drive to local schools, businesses, churches, and clubs. It can help to set a goal like, "We need to collect 250 pounds of dry pet food." The most important thing to remember is that every bit of pet food you collect helps. If you only collect 100 pounds of pet food that is still huge! That small amount can make a difference throughout the month for a senior and their pet.

Adopt-a-Resident Project

> "I feel like if you're a really good human being, you can try to find something beautiful in every single person, no matter what."
>
> –Lady Gaga

THIS PROGRAM PAIRS nursing home seniors low on family with families willing to adopt them. Over 90 percent of our local nursing home seniors have less than one family visit per month. Can you imagine that? Loneliness is a common problem. We get these seniors adopted by families who will remember them on birthdays and major holidays. These small acts of kindness change their whole world.

Adoption doesn't necessarily mean a face-to-face visit. Our Adopt-a-Resident Project is mostly done through the mail. It doesn't cost much to send a greeting card on major holidays or to mail a birthday card. It also isn't hard to send a tiny little treat once or twice a year. That's what we ask adoptive families to do. We want to make sure no birthday is forgotten and that everyone is remembered in some small way on the big days like Christmas, Valentine's Day, and Thanksgiving.

I know a senior who was born right before Christmas. The last time I checked I think he was ninety-nine years old. Well,

sadly, one Christmas Jimmie's family completely forgot his birthday. No one called or came by and not a single family member mailed him a card. I guess there was something silly in my head that assumed that ninety-nine-year-olds kind of outgrew the birthday celebration thing. I think I actually thought people that age didn't care if anyone remembered their birthdays. Jimmie showed me that I was really wrong about that. Jimmie was sad on his birthday and he was still sad a month later. He didn't want to eat much and some days he didn't even want to get out of bed. The one thing that saved the day was our adoption program! Even though Jimmie's real family forgot his birthday, his adoptive family remembered!! Jimmie had also hit the jackpot when it came to the people who adopted him. We always tell people they can go as big or as little as they want with gifts and cards for the residents. The family that adopted Jimmie was the best of the best. They sent him a box of his favorite treats and an Arkansas Razorback hat. No matter how sad he was about his family, he would always smile when he put on that hat. Someone remembered and it didn't matter who. Jimmie was not forgotten after all and someone out there loved him.

HOW DID ADOPT-A-RESIDENT GET STARTED?

I met a nursing home resident named Shannon when I was ten years old. Sharon had lived in the nursing home for nine years and never had a visitor. She didn't even get cards on her birthday and her Thanksgiving was spent with nursing home staff. No family came to see her even on the "important" days.

You could tell she had no family because her room was bare. Residents who have family tend to have rooms filled with personal photos of grandkids,

children, art, homemade quilts, and all kinds of trinkets lying around that scream out "I am loved." People like Sharon have rooms that look blank, empty, and bland. It takes three seconds to spot the difference.

I felt Sharon's pain and I wanted to do something to change the world for people like her, so I created an adoption program. That way residents like Sharon would have rooms filled with little signs of life and love given to them by their adoptive families.

PROBLEM SOLVED!

Anyone can adopt a nursing home resident. We have hundreds of residents wanting to be adopted and over one thousand adopted across the United States. What does adoption mean? It simply means you agree to mail them a card on birthdays and holidays and send a small treat once or twice a year.

I have a sheet of fun facts on each resident who needs to be adopted. It has their favorite snacks like chocolate or pork-n-beans, shoe size, favorite color, favorite activity, and, of course, their birthday! I share these fun facts with the families who want to adopt a resident. I ask them to pledge to adopt for one year and then they can stop or select a new resident.

This program has been successful at ending those bare rooms because we ask people to mail photos of their kids, pets, and vacations. We ask for pretty quilts and pillows, and we make sure these items fill the empty rooms. I watched Sharon's room turn into the most loved room of all! It didn't matter that the photos were not her grandkids or her pets. She didn't care at all. The photos and personal items showed the world she was loved.

Hey victor. I wrote to you about a month ago, and I just wanted to check up on you. I hope everything is going good in your life, and that youre happy 😊 Please continue Being the cool person you are, and Dont let anyone tell You Different.

Sinceraly, your friend Ashton

Adopted residents love handwritten letters.

YOU CAN DO IT, TOO!

People want to help these seniors. On our website and social media, we make announcements throughout the year and ask people to email us if they want to adopt. We ask essential staff to email us if they have a resident low on family or funds, too. It's a super popular project. We had approximately 500 seniors adopted the first time we launched it.

If you would like to try to adopt a resident in your community, you can start by calling the nursing home. Nursing home staff are useful for spotting what is needed and for knowing which residents are low on family. If the facility is interested in your help, they will help you gather the information you need; if they can't help, they will usually tell you which staff member can. Don't always expect a reply right away. Staff members at long-term care facilities are busy. Be patient because they will get back to you and do their very best to help us help the residents. The hardest part is breaking through that first time, but once they see what you can do, they will always help you make their lives better if the need is there.

If you don't have any luck adopting a resident locally, be sure to reach out to our nonprofit organization. We can connect you with a resident in need of adoption.

Send our staff an email at 3wishesforruby@gmail.com to sign up for the Adopt-a-Resident Project. We will pair you with the perfect senior. You might also want to check with nursing facilities in your area to see if they have an adoption program.

Three Wishes for Whiskers

> "Time spent with cats is never wasted."
>
> –Sigmund Freud

THIS IS A PROGRAM that not only pairs senior shelter cats with seniors in a nursing home but also helps seniors take care of the pets they already own! We scour local pet shelters for the perfect older cat companions for our seniors, and we find them a fur-ever home at a nursing facility. We also keep seniors supplied with all the pet food they will ever need to make sure that none of their pets go hungry. The project also provides Pet Meals on Wheels to homebound seniors struggling to feed their pets.

Mature cats come with a personality and a card describing their habits so you know exactly what you're getting.

HOW DID THREE WISHES FOR WHISKERS GET STARTED?

It started with the "cat lady." I was ten years old when I met Henrietta and she was in her eighties. She lived in a nursing home. She said there was never a day in her life when she didn't have a cat. She was very quick to tell me that "God put me here to take care of the cats." There were dozens of stray cats living outside her room at the nursing home. She loved to care for them all. Henrietta taught me how much pets mean to people like her. Henrietta introduced me to the cats that lived outside the nursing home. She had named them all, mostly by color, and she showed me what they needed. It gets very cold in the mountains where we live and the cats didn't have winter shelter. They also didn't have a steady source of food. They needed Henrietta and they needed a little help from me, too!

PROBLEM SOLVED!

Henrietta inspired me to start a project called Three Wishes for Whiskers. I'm always on the lookout for the perfect cat for nursing home seniors, visiting pet

Cats can make seniors very happy! This is Hope and was our first Three Wishes for Whiskers kitty cat!

loves the residents like mad.

Another example is Elvis, a mature cat we adopted from a shelter. He was a take-back (someone adopted him and brought him back). We call him the friendliest cat in Arkansas because he hugs our residents with one paw around each side of their neck and he will stay that way for an hour. He is the ultimate lap cat and if there was a contest for lap-sitting, he would win the world record easily.

I found Elvis on one of my trips to the pet shelter. He was one of only three cats left for adoption. Elvis was skinny and needed to be brushed. His hair was thin and his coat was dull. He was not pretty, but, guess what? Elvis jumped up and hugged my neck with each paw. He sat there for a few minutes just holding me. I was going to the shelter to pick a cat and instead, a cat picked me!

We adopted Elvis for our nursing home seniors, and he lives in our nonprofit's public community center. People come from all over to visit, and they smile so BIG when they meet the kind-of-famous Elvis. I also take Elvis with me to the nursing home. Seniors can pet him through the cat pack and listen to him purr. The residents' faces light up when they see Elvis. It's magical.

Elvis is one of the many adult cats we

shelters to check out their older cats. I tell the workers that I am looking for a cat that's a little bit lazy and wants to be held all the time. The shelter employees really know the cats inside and out and will recommend the right cat. It's my job to find a nursing home that will make it their forever pet. This is how Three Wishes for Whiskers works. We match senior cats with seniors!

One of our first mature cats, Sweetie, was skipped over for four years before we adopted her. She is a jolly green-eyed giant, and a little lazy, which I love. She drools a tiny bit when residents rub her chin. Her favorite things are sleep and humans (in that order) and she have adopted for seniors through the Three Wishes for Whiskers Project. We have given many rescue cats like Elvis fur-ever homes in nursing homes. I've learned that senior citizens miss their pets a ton and when we give them a cat, it can change their lives. Besides, what cat wouldn't love to live in a home with 100+ grandmas and grandpas? I'd call that a match made in heaven.

It's time to rethink the whole concept of adopting pets. Mature cats come with a personality and a card describing their habits so you know exactly what you are getting. They don't care how long you are at school and they are never going to make you feel guilty when you've had a super-busy week. They come fully house-trained, spayed or neutered, and are past the dreaded supervising, biting, and scratching-furniture phases. It's like someone else did all the hard work for you!

YOU CAN DO IT, TOO!

Call a local nursing facility and ask if they have pet needs. Host a pet food drive or check a local animal shelter for a senior cat who needs adoption. Don't hesitate to share the pet on social media and let people know this might be the purr-fect pet for a lonely senior. Check with local nursing homes and assisted living facilities and don't forget to ask if they need help with pet food.

We Make a Difference!

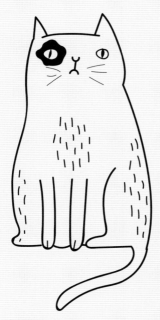

I can't give residents their families back and I sure can't make their families come visit them. I can, however, put a cat in their laps and I can make sure they never go without pet food. Eighty percent of nursing home residents feel lonely. Pets are a great way to combat that feeling!

The Cat Lady's Torch

TRULY, THE THIRD sentence out of Henrietta's mouth was, "God put me at this nursing home to take care of the cats." It didn't take long to realize that she wasn't kidding.

When I met Henrietta at the nursing home she wouldn't speak to me until she had her lipstick on. She told me all about the cats that lived outside her room. Most of us would call them "colony cats," but to Henrietta they were much more. They were her best friends.

Henrietta and I joined forces to trap the cats and have them each spayed or neutered. It was a sight to behold. Henrietta stooped over in a wheelchair speaking "magic cat talk" and actually getting these feral cats into a carrier. She lured them all, one by one, and soon she had them tamed and eating from our hands.

> "Cats rule the world."
>
> —Jim Davis

A dynamite team for our furry friends.

She would call for help when one was sick or ask for help feeding them when she wasn't feeling well. We kept them stocked with food and gave them good housing. Henrietta was their saving grace. If you visit the facility today, years later, you will no longer see feral cats but rather tamed fluff balls who seek love and cat food at every turn of the tail. It's a real-life Catopia for the seniors who live here and a huge labor of love from Henrietta.

We recently knew something was wrong at the facility because the cats were unsettled. Henrietta's favorite, Little Gray, was circling the feet of a man in a wheelchair and he didn't just want food, he wanted love. We went back inside and saw with our own eyes what we already knew in our hearts. Henrietta, the Cat Lady, was gone. Her room was empty.

We knew we had to pass the cat torch to someone who would love and care for these cats like Henrietta did. We asked a few residents to take over the cats and they said no but told us to "Check with that man at the end of the hall." That's when we found Michael, a spunky, retired Navy veteran who loved to feed the cats. He had shared his own lunch with the cats right before we came because cat food can be kind of hard to come by in a nursing home. We gave Michael a giant bag of cat food and a kind nurse informed him that he was taking the cat torch from Henrietta. We had a new cat "lady" named Michael.

To our sweet Henrietta Graham, the ultimate cat lady, you will always be in our hearts and we promise to keep passing the Cat Lady's Torch for life.

Upcycle Art Project

"One man's trash is another man's treasure."

–English Proverb

LET'S BE REALLY HONEST here. Where do your little art papers from school really end up? Maybe they end up on a family bulletin board or a refrigerator for a few months? Then what? Do they end up in the trash? I think it's very normal for most student art to end up in landfills at some point. You know who would love this art? Nursing home seniors. It has always surprised me just how much seniors love drawings from kids. There are many times that a senior's favorite gift from us is a simple drawing. It doesn't matter if the art is from a talented art student or if it's a scribble of colors from my brother, they treasure the art all the same.

This is worth more than gold to a senior.

Smile sacks! Nursing home seniors love the art!

HOW DID UPCYCLE ART GET STARTED?

This project actually got started by accident. We give most of our little wishes inside paper lunch sacks that have been decorated by kids. The sacks are really cute and they have kind messages, hearts, and happy art on the outside. One summer, we had an actual kid artist who helped us decorate the lunch sacks. She could only volunteer for us in the summer so we knew her last day was in August and her beautiful, artistic sacks would stop!

Well, the following year I found four empty paper lunch sacks made by this artist in a nursing home resident's room. The resident had cherished this art so much that she kept it for a solid year! I thought about my little brother's art and how much student art is thrown in the trash. I see kids' art in the trash all the time. It's not a bad thing but I think if they knew it could change a life, they would put it in a crate for us to upcycle

This resident was so happy to receive the gumball tree art. It brightened her whole room because the walls had been bare.

projects for seniors. Lots of times during big holidays like Christmas and Valentine's Day, the students will send the seniors beautiful themed art pages. It gives a purpose to their art.

instead of trashing it.

It didn't take long to put together a plan. That is what I do. I see a problem, like lonely seniors and art being thrown in the trash, and I come up with a solution. My solution was to ask local parents, daycares, schools, and art teachers to save any unwanted art for us. Soon we began receiving hundreds of pieces of student art each week. We upcycle every piece back to a senior who needs to be cheered up. It works like magic. It also teaches elementary students how easy it can be for them to give back and help others. I have had several kindergarten teachers tell me how much students enjoy creating art

PROBLEM SOLVED!

We have talked about lots of small things that nursing home seniors need—books, wishes, pets, and pet food. How to fulfill a wish for a senior who just wants to feel less alone? That's a little bit harder because it is not like they need you to run out to the store to buy some soda for them. They are asking you for love and attention.

One of the best ways for nursing home seniors to feel less alone is through upcycling children's art. Picasso said, "Every child is an artist" and that is so true in the eyes of a lonely senior. They think the art is just for them. It makes them feel good inside and out. They can also put it up in their room and use it as a daily reminder that someone loves them.

The Upcycle Art Project also helps save our planet, which is something I love! Did you know that schools in America consume an average of 32 billion sheets of paper a year? How many trees would that be? I know not all of this paper is art, but I think it's a good chunk of it. It's nice to think that we are keeping the paper out of the landfills and using it to make a senior happy!

reach out to schools in your district like the high school, middle school, and local colleges. You might be able to collect lots of art this way. Don't forget about daycares, summer camps, and churches. They also have youth groups that can donate art.

I think any nursing home would be happy to accept your art donations. You could simply drop it off at the door to the attention of the "Activity Director." Be sure to "spread the wealth" and donate the art to as many facilities as possible.

YOU CAN DO IT, TOO!

Upcycling art for seniors is a project that anyone can do. A great place to start is your school. Offer to put a basket in your classroom so students can donate any art projects they don't want. Ask your art teacher to do the same. Maybe your school has assemblies once a month where all the students gather? Ask to speak to the school about collecting art for seniors. Suggest that teachers make special art projects on big days like Valentine's Day, Christmas, and Thanksgiving just to be used for local nursing home seniors.

If you want to go a little bigger,

A STUDENT'S ART WARMED HIS HEART.

Senior Pen Pal Project

"I've learned . . . the best classroom in the world is at the feet of an elderly person"

-Andy Rooney

HAVE YOU EVER HEARD OF A pen pal? Pen pals are people who communicate with each other over a long distance. It's usually done through the old-fashioned mail and our seniors love real mail! But, we also expanded our pen pal project to include emails, social media messages, and classroom videos from students across America. Our Senior Pen Pal Project brings back the excitement of mail, for sure, but it's no ordinary pen pal program. It's a pen pal program with a modern twist.

This resident is so happy when she wakes up to real mail!

Long-term care facilities hold some of the greatest treasures in America. Why do I say that? These facilities have senior citizens who can tell us what it was like to live during times that the rest of us can only read about in school.

Our seniors were alive when Martin Luther King Jr. marched and some of our senior women were real-life Rosie the Riveters! They fought in wars, hid out in trenches, and lived without computers, video games, and the Internet.

I have met veterans who can share stories of Pearl Harbor, Vietnam, and D-Day. I met a woman who grew up in Germany and would often see the infamous Adolf Hitler take a tour of her elementary school. I met women who had to heat their bath water on a fire and go to the bathroom in something called an outhouse because they just didn't have running water for most of their lives. I have met men who ate duck eggs because there were times in America when food was scarce.

If you stop to think of all the things that have been invented in the last hundred years, it is pretty remarkable. What can you think of that has been invented in your lifetime? Social media? Game consoles? For our seniors and their generation, they saw airplanes, automobiles, paved highways, computers, and refrigerators invented. They witnessed health-care changes like the invention of antibiotics and vaccines. Lots of my nursing home friends rode to school on a horse. That is no joke.

They have so many stories they can share with you. I love to ask them questions about what it was like to live back then. They love to share their stories with others and the Senior Pen Pal Project is a great way to do that.

HOW DID THE SENIOR PEN PAL PROJECT GET STARTED?

I love to hear stories of the nursing home seniors' lives. I wanted other kids in America to have a chance to learn from them, too. My nursing home friend Virginia told the best stories. She ran a hose over 200 feet from a spring in the ground to her kitchen sink. This is how she was able to get "running water." Her stories were much more interesting than a history class and even better than reading a history book!

I've learned so much about history from my senior friends. I interviewed a man who was 103 years old! His name was Campbell. I had lots of questions that I wanted to ask him mainly because he was so very old. I asked him what the best invention of his lifetime was. Do you want to guess what he told me? It's actually a hard question for people like him to answer because so many amazing things were invented during his life.

The washing machine, ice box (freezer), the refrigerator, air conditioning, computers, and major highways were all invented during his life! He thought the best invention of his lifetime was the automobile. He said that he grew up in rural Arkansas and it was very difficult for older boys to finish school during that time because their parents needed the boys to work on their farms, not be in school. He said in order to finish high school, he rode a horse to a school thirty miles away. He didn't get a car until he was in his thirties, but it did change lives. It was easier for people to travel and get the things they needed.

I was also very curious about what some of Campbell's best memories would be. Once you live to be 100, what memories stand out? For me it might be getting my first dog, losing my first tooth, or going to Disney World. But Campbell's answer surprised me. He told me that his favorite memory was collecting pocket watches and traveling in a camper with his wife. That is pretty incredible when you think about it. I bet he had thousands of memories over his lifetime and he chose those two as the best of all—pocket watches and traveling in a camper.

Some of the adults in my nonprofit organization loved these stories and they wanted to find a way to share them with school kids. The seniors also told me they loved sharing their wisdom, history, and stories with kids. We asked local students to be pen pals with our seniors and we also had some kids from as far away as Texas send seniors questions to answer, like "Have you ever seen a unicorn?" and "Did you go to kindergarten?" Guess what? Most seniors in their eighties or older didn't go to kindergarten because it didn't exist when they were in school! Sharing this knowledge was fun and I'm pretty sure students and seniors learned something new.

I love to get emails from teachers across America who have a question or two for a senior about a certain time in history. I know a lady who was born in 1918, the same year that women earned the right to vote. I also knew a resident who was a Rosie the Riveter. The story behind Rosie the Riveter is that during World War II many men in America were called into the military and this left our factories and shipyards low on employees. Women began to take these jobs! They called the women who started to work in what used to be a "man's job" Rosie the Riveters. I met one! These are the types of people that our nonprofit can connect you with! Wouldn't that be fun? What would you ask them?

PROBLEM SOLVED!

The 1.4 million seniors living in America's nursing homes have so much knowledge and incredible stories about history to share with us. The Senior Pen Pal Project is a great way to access that knowledge and unleash tons of wisdom that can be useful in our own lives.

YOU CAN DO IT, TOO!

Do you want to write a letter to a senior? Do you want to know what it was like to be alive during the Pearl Harbor attack or maybe you are just dying to know if any of our ninety-year-olds have actually seen a UFO? Ask us.

It's super easy to send a letter or ask a question. Our email is 3wishesforruby@gmail.com and you can send any classroom or student questions to that email.

You or your classroom can join our pen pal program by just sticking a letter in the mail a few times a year. We will make sure it gets to a senior in need. The website to download instructions is www.3wishes.global or have an adult send us an email at 3wishesforruby@gmail.com and we will help you.

Send those letters and make a difference!

Postcards of Kindness

> "Carry out a random act of kindness, with no expectation of reward, safe in the knowledge that one day someone might do the same for you"
>
> – Princess Diana

WHAT IS A POSTCARD? It's those smallish cards used for sending a message through the mail. The card usually has a photograph or art on one side and the stamp costs less than a usual postage stamp. You can find postcards in any place that sells souvenirs. Sometimes the postcards can be really funny and I've seen others with pictures of the Grand Canyon and touristy places like that. I love postcards and I love how cheap and easy they are to use.

This resident was so happy to get a postcard in the mail! She is one of the residents who checked for mail daily!

Postcards of Kindness is a project that connects people, anyone, to nursing home seniors across America and gives them a way to mail an anonymous postcard with a kind message to a nursing home senior. When someone says "mail" to me, I think of "email," and I don't use email often. I prefer to text, call, or FaceTime. Most Americans have a cellphone, but most nursing home seniors do not. That is one reason why seniors feel so lonely nowadays. They don't have the Internet or can't use it correctly. They still rely on things like mail and phone calls to stay in touch, send love, and wish people a "happy birthday" or a "Merry Christmas."

My dad is pretty serious about checking the mail. He hardly ever misses a day checking the mailbox. I don't understand it at all. He only seems to get junk mail, catalogs, and bills. My mom says that when she was growing up, one of her chores was to walk a quarter of a mile to check the mailbox for her family. She said it was a really big deal. The family knew exactly when the mail was supposed to arrive and they expected my mom to be up at the mailbox during that hour to collect it.

Mom was excited to go through the mail because people wrote lots of letters back then. They sent cards, birthday greetings, and little letters to update others on what was going on in their lives. They didn't have social media or emails then, so mail was one of the best ways to communicate. Mail was something to look forward to and it was exciting because you never knew what treasures you would find in the mailbox!

Mail is important to seniors and postcards are a perfect way to make a senior smile and give them something to show friends, staff, and visitors all week. Postcards make it easy to spread kindness to nursing home seniors.

HOW DID POSTCARDS OF KINDNESS GET STARTED?

If I happened to be in a nursing home after lunch, I would see a stream of residents in wheelchairs headed up to the front office. One day I followed them and I found out that they were checking with the front office to see if any mail came for them. They were wheeling up there with excitement and hope on their faces and some would return kind of serious and a little sad. I can't tell you a single time that I saw a resident receive mail when I was there. I could see that not getting mail made them sad and lonely. That was a problem and I knew I could solve it by rallying my supporters across the country.

PROBLEM SOLVED!

I created a social media page that lists photos and addresses of nursing homes across America that will accept anonymous postcards with kind messages on them. It was an instant hit in our nursing homes in Arkansas. The residents who wheeled up to the front to check the mail would be given one of these postcards of kindness. It made their entire day. They didn't care who it was from or why they received it. They were just thrilled that someone thought enough about them to write a little note. It was such an easy way to relieve some of their loneliness and it only costs about fifty cents.

Some of the postcards included photos from someone's vacation. I saw a lot of beach photos on postcards and I was shocked to learn that many of the nursing home seniors had never seen the beach! I saw some postcards from Stonehenge in England and the Golden Gate Bridge. The residents would carry them around all day. The photos gave them a reason to socialize with other people and they gave them a good story to tell. The very, very, very best part of the postcards was that they gave them a reason to smile. The seniors felt loved and you could see it all over their faces.

This nursing home in Arkansas posts all the Postcards of Kindness on the wall for the residents to see!

YOU CAN DO IT, TOO!

Anyone can send a postcard. If you visit our Facebook group Postcards of Kindness-USA, you will find a list of nursing home addresses in America that accept anonymous postcards. How does this work? You write a kind message on a cute postcard and mail it to the nursing home address on the Facebook page. The staff will give the postcard to the resident who needs a boost that day. Maybe someone has been sick, has lost a loved one, or is just having a bad week. The staff will use the postcard to cheer them up! It's OK if you sign your name on the card and tell them about yourself. We don't expect the residents to write back with this program but sometimes they do! Be creative. They love postcards that they can use to tell a story to their friends.

The Three Wishes Community Center (Vintage Skills)

> "Teach me and I'll forget. Show me and I may remember. Involve me and I will learn"
>
> —Benjamin Franklin

OUR NONPROFIT HAS an amazing community center where people my age can connect and interact with senior citizens of all kinds. We have huge crafting tables, murals, art, and games. And our seniors who visit the center love to share their knowledge of vintage skills.

What are vintage skills? Older people think of these skills as "practical skills." They are old-fashioned skills like sewing, knitting, cooking from scratch, and gardening. Not too long ago these were skills that people thought were necessary for everyone to know a little bit about.

A classroom of children at the Three Wishes Community Center

I don't know how to sew but thanks to many of my senior friends, I know a lot about cooking, knitting, and gardening. I'm so glad they shared their knowledge with me!

HOW DID THE THREE WISHES COMMUNITY CENTER GET STARTED?

Who owns 2,000 pairs of socks? Me! My nonprofit fulfills small wishes for nursing home seniors across America, so we store lots of items that seniors need. Here is a funny story about my socks. I was a GoFundMe Kid Hero in 2019 and my story went viral. I didn't expect that to happen at all. A video of my work was viewed over 50 million times. I mentioned needing socks, candy, and small treats in the video, and in a very short amount of time, I had amassed a warehouse of these small wish items for seniors.

We started to store the socks in my house at first, not knowing how huge this would become. It got to the point that my whole family had to turn sideways to walk down the hallways. We had wishes stacked from floor to ceiling in every possible place in our house. The items kept coming in the mail, so we moved everything to a huge barn at my grandfather's house.

We had thousands of candy bars, baby dolls, meal substitutes, shampoo, and bags of pet food. It was an amazing sight of love for nursing home seniors from all over the world. We received wishes from the North Pole, Alaska, and as far as Brighton, United Kingdom.

And the support just kept coming. I knew I would need a space to call my own outside of my grandfather's barn. We found an amazing old building on the square in the downtown area of my hometown. The property was over a hundred years old. People told me that it used to be a general store back in the day.

The building needed a lot of work. My family and the whole community pitched in to get the space ready for our cause. I found artists to paint incredible murals inside and out. I picked out giant pictures of senior citizens to put on the walls. It became the space of my dreams, but guess what? It was too big.

I thought about my favorite nursing home seniors as I tried to figure out what to do with all of the extra space. I remembered many of the things they taught me over the years and I thought about their stories. They explained to me what the term "vintage skills" meant.

A great example of a vintage skill is when my nursing home friend Henrietta taught me about vegetable gardening, cross-pollination, and plant compatibility. So I built the seniors a garden and I was going to plant tomatoes and corn together. Henrietta explained why this combination was a bad idea. She told me that they would compete for nutrients and sun and outgrow the small area we had for them. I was blown away by all of her knowledge of gardening.

My senior friend Wilma is 102 years old and she is a walking textbook of vintage skills. Wilma taught us how to make homemade butter. Her family made it all the time when she was growing up in the 1920s. They also stored their meats miles away from their home in a "smokehouse." They didn't have refrigerators, so the meat was smoked so that it would last longer. Life was a lot different back then.

I love to create activities where kids my age and seniors can get together and share stories. One of my very favorite things to do with seniors is show-and-tell. I get together five people my age with five seniors. Each of us brings a show-and-tell item and guess what? We all learn something. We might show some seniors who a superhero is or how to play UNO. They have shown us things like a Purple Heart award won for

Accessible garden beds are the best.

bravery while serving in the military, an antique necklace from Guatemala, or a piece of mysterious rock that one senior was sure came from a UFO.

We do show-and-tell a little different because some of our seniors aren't able to bring an item to show, so we just let them tell a story. I like to tell people that instead of show-and-tell, we have show *or* tell. It's a perfect way to share stories and it's a lot of fun.

PROBLEM SOLVED!

The large space in the front of our new building is now a community center. Our goal is to connect kids with seniors. We hire seniors from the community as staff. We have seniors teach all kinds of vintage skills. On any given day, we are hosting school groups, free crafting days, and homeschool classes.

YOU CAN DO IT, TOO!

You don't need a community center to teach vintage skills, host a show-and-tell, or share stories. Anytime you come across a senior in your family or out in your community who knows a lot about a vintage skill, you can ask them to show you how to do it. Wedding or church events or Grandparents' Day at your school are all good times to suggest a show-and-tell story swap, or to ask a senior to teach a vintage skill. It doesn't matter if it's one senior teaching one kid or twenty kids. The important part is that we are making sure the knowledge our seniors have doesn't fade away.

Hygiene Kits

> "Life's most persistent and urgent question is, 'What are you doing for others?'"
>
> -Martin Luther King Jr.

I'M GUESSING YOUR morning or night routine involves using some type of hygiene product. These are basic items that we all typically use to stay clean. When I think of hygiene products, I think of shampoo, conditioner, body soap, deodorant, toothpaste, and lotion. These are basics. I can't imagine not having all my favorites or wondering if I will have enough toothpaste to last the whole month.

I know seniors who experience this fear and go without some of these hygiene items that the rest of us might take for granted. The amount of assistance with hygiene products totally depends on what type of facility the senior lives in. I always ask seniors if they have what they need to stay clean and, sadly, many tell me no. This is why our nonprofit began giving out hygiene kits to seniors in long-term care.

HOW DID HYGIENE KITS GET STARTED?

I would see seniors in the nursing home playing bingo to win something called "bingo bucks." I thought it was pretty cool until I realized that they were using these "bingo bucks" to buy basics like shampoo, a decent bar of soap, and good toothpaste. I remember asking myself,

"Why would a senior choose toothpaste over a candy bar?" I thought the soap they were given would work fine. I was wrong.

I spoke to the lady in charge of bingo and I asked her for a list of the most common products the seniors used their "bingo bucks" for. They were mainly using them for basic hygiene products. I also learned something else that I must admit I now find to be embarrassing. I didn't think "older ladies" wore makeup. Boy, was I wrong. Many seniors used their "bingo bucks" for lipstick, facial lotion, hairspray, and blush. It doesn't matter how old you are, people still have the desire to look their best. Makeup and face care were considered an "extra." They were items that weren't provided for by the facility and therefore it was expected to be purchased out of their small monthly allowance. Let's stop for a second and do a math problem.

Betty is a nursing home senior who receives a monthly allowance of $40 to spend on personal items. She has no family and no other source of income. Betty has made a list of things she needs to buy in one month:

Here is one of my hygiene kits for a female! This is our storage room at the Three Wishes Community Center where we keep all of our wish items. I even throw in a little lipstick (Henrietta taught me that).

Moisturizing body soap	$3.00
Brand name deodorant	$5.00
Haircut	$15.00
New toothpaste	$4.00
Lipstick	$5.00
Better lotion for dry skin	$7.00

How much money does Betty have left over? My calculations show me that Betty would have one dollar left over.

This is just money Betty wants to spend on hygiene. She hasn't spent a dollar on things like cellphone service, Internet service, socks, or shoes. What if Betty has other needs? You might remember when I told you that one of my very first residents in the Three Wishes Project only asked me for "pants that fit."

This is how that happens.

I decided to add hygiene and makeup items to our local "list of needs." I asked people to donate products to us when they could and I used the money I had raised to purchase the items.

I want to clarify something. Seniors in a nursing home do receive free hygiene products. But the products they receive free are standard medical brand. I have used the lotion and it's watery. It is "meh," especially if your skin is really dry and itchy. The toothpaste and shampoo are the same. I love a good bargain, but I do need hygiene products that work.

The seniors living in low-income apartments, assisted living, and retirement centers don't even get the free stuff. They are responsible for acquiring all of their hygiene products, including Band-Aids and toilet paper. It's a lot to think about.

PROBLEM SOLVED!

With the hygiene products, I do not buy the fanciest brands but I make sure they are brands with good reviews. In addition to lotion, toothpaste, shampoo, and makeup, here is a list of other products I collect for seniors in long-term care:

    Conditioner
    Deodorant (spray and solid)
    Liquid body wash
    Hand sanitizer
    Band-Aids
    Toilet paper, paper towels
    Hairspray
    Combs

Access to GOOD hygiene products is a community effort that makes life a little easier for seniors. When they don't have to spend their small allowance on these basics, it frees them up to buy a takeout meal, their favorite beverage, or maybe pay a bill. It's an impactful way to help seniors in long-term care.

YOU CAN DO IT, TOO!

Hygiene Kits is a project for lower-income seniors that can be done once or several times throughout the year. Call around and find a long-term care facility in your community whose residents could use help with these common hygiene products.

Ask for an approximate number needed for each of the items above. Next, host a "hygiene kit" drive in your community. Use the tools and tips that we talked about with book drives and pet food drives. Make sure you have somewhere with enough space to store the products. Remember, the facility that is accepting your help will have residents who are very embarrassed that they can't afford to buy their own shampoo. Make sure you don't share the name of the facility you are helping. You can just say, "I am helping seniors in a local retirement center or nursing home."

Leo's LEGO®s

"We don't stop
playing because we
grow old; we grow
old because we
stop playing."

**–George
Bernard Shaw**

WHO LIKES TO stay busy? It's almost like we can never get too bored anymore. I mean, we have phones and constant notifications around us all the time. This isn't true for nursing home seniors, who don't typically use any type of electronic device. Nursing home seniors definitely get bored. Have you ever stopped to think about how they cure their boredom without electronic devices?

Leo's Lego Boxes for Seniors

Three Wishes for Ruby's Residents is a nonprofit organization fulfilling small wishes to seniors

Free local pick-up for verified LTC staff

IT'S A BUSY BOX FOR SENIORS

SENIORS PLAY WITH LEGOS, TOO.

I can tell you what I see the seniors doing. Some of this we have already talked about, like reading books and receiving real letters in the mail. But they also like a good board or card game. Many of these seniors used to "tinker" with things all the time when they lived outside of a nursing home. The men tell me that they worked on car engines, picked vegetables from a garden, or worked in a factory putting things together. The ladies tell me similar ways that they were always using their hands. The ladies used to sew, craft, can vegetables, and shell peas. My point is that they were busy people and their hands did a lot of their busy work.

HOW DID LEO'S LEGOS GET STARTED?

My friend and kid board member, Leo, came up with an idea to give a few seniors Lego building blocks. I have to admit that, at first, I wasn't sure this would work. I tried to picture an eighty-year-old playing with Legos and it didn't seem like a good fit. I was wrong! Leo put an assortment of his old Legos inside a cute little tackle box. We gave the box to a nursing home senior who used to work on cars. The seniors looked puzzled at first but we showed him all the little things he could build with the Lego pieces.

The box was perfect for an old mechanic because it has car parts, axles,

I wonder what he will create today?

wheels, and all sorts of pieces that can be used to build a Lego car or truck. Sure enough, James caught on to the Legos and he spent the next hour making the coolest car you've ever seen. It had so much detail and thought put into it. James was able to use his hands and his mind to create something unique. He was so proud of himself and, believe it or not, nursing home seniors don't get a lot of opportunities to beam with pride. Think about it: usually, people are making and doing things for them. That's kind of why they are in a nursing home, to begin with. The Lego box opened new doors for the seniors.

Leo's Legos became a modern "busy box" for seniors. It allows them to use their hands and minds, and express their creativity. I love how the seniors will show off their creations to staff and friends. It is always a very happy smile along with something like "Look what I made today." I love to see the seniors proud of themselves and I really love seeing them happy.

Most nursing homes have therapy departments that are used to help seniors regain function in their arms, hands, or legs after a major illness. We noticed that the therapists loved our Leo's Legos boxes, too. The therapists were able to use the boxes to help strengthen people's hands and fingers.

The speech therapists also liked the boxes to help seniors use their minds to build and sort colors and shapes. The Lego boxes became a useful tool and fun activity that could be used throughout the nursing home.

One last way that I have seen the Lego boxes being used is by visiting kids! These are seniors, so of course there are grandkids and great-grandkids who come inside the nursing homes to visit. It can be hard to keep the little kids entertained while the older parents visit with their loved one. If the little kids are super bored, the visit with the senior might get cut short and that is no fun at all for the senior. We let staff share our Lego boxes with any kids who visit. The kids also love to build things with the pieces and because the tackle box is so easy to carry around, the kids can use the box right inside the senior's room. The seniors love to watch the kids play. I think sometimes we all think that to "visit" someone inside a nursing home we have to talk. You really don't. Seniors love to watch life happen. It's hard to describe the joy seniors experience from watching one of their little grandkids play with something like Legos inside their room. It definitely makes the whole visit more enjoyable and a little longer, too!

PROBLEM SOLVED!

Nursing home seniors get bored. It can be hard to fill a sixteen-hour day when you don't have distractions like phones, tons of visitors, and the Internet. There are so many activities that seniors love, like reading, puzzles, DVDs, board games, and music. My friends and I have also discovered that we can take a modern toy like Legos and turn it into a meaningful activity for seniors. It's just one more way we can help a senior smile, stay busy, and create something they can be proud of!

YOU CAN DO IT, TOO!

Just remember nursing home seniors the next time your family wants to downsize their Lego collection. You could put some great car, airplane, and wheel pieces inside a small tackle box and give one or two boxes to each nursing home in your area. One to three boxes per facility is usually enough.

You could even suggest a Lego building contest and make it a challenge for the seniors. The seniors could make their best "creation" and put it on display for the staff to vote on their favorite! There are lots of ways to make this a fun project for the seniors living near you.

I never thought my hobby of helping seniors would be admired by other kids. But I have learned that kindness is contagious and that seniors are adored by so many of us. This next chapter features testimonials from a few of my friends whose kind hearts are impacting seniors in their communities. They inspire me and I hope that they might inspire you too.

3

Inspired by Kindness

AVA GRAYCE

My name is Ava Grayce and I'm a high school student from Baton Rouge, Louisiana. Working with Ruby is one of the best things I think I've done.

I was always one to think that people were deserving of kindness and I could never understand why there would be a lack of it anywhere. To me, getting to share kindness with the elderly is something that I wish I had done so much earlier. But even so, I will do it as long as I can and bring others to do it as well.

I've been working with seniors at various nursing homes and assisted living facilities in Louisiana, in the Gonzales, Baton Rouge, and False River areas. Recently I got to partner with McDonald's to provide Happy Meals for each of the residents. It was a joy getting to see how happy they all were and they seemed to love seeing new faces.

I typically go to places with my kitten, Atticus the Catticus, and he helps bring a smile to residents' faces. I enjoy getting to talk with residents and play bingo with them. When I visit nursing homes, sometimes I bring Smile Sacks. These are little gift bags with goodies inside. The residents will fill out forms asking what snacks they like and we will provide everything we can. The residents we

work with love the Smile Sacks and we love getting to bring them and see how happy it makes them.

Originally, I started out with an assisted living facility in Gonzales. I was nervous, antsy, and, frankly, didn't want to be there all summer. I very quickly changed my mind after getting to talk with the residents. I became more comfortable talking with them and simply enjoying their company. They all loved getting to meet Atticus and playing with him. As time went on, and after seeing Ruby Kate herself work in a nursing home when I visited Arkansas, I decided to visit more places.

One experience I believe was very helpful was when I visited a place where there were primarily dementia patients. I was so nervous and scared to go, but I thoroughly enjoyed the residents regardless of that.

I wanted to continue doing all this but there are still a few things I need to work on, such as speaking louder and being more confident. Still, from giving out Smile Sacks to working with McDonald's or just visiting residents, this whole opportunity has been such a delight and I encourage other people to start doing it as well.

LEO GAETA

My first experience in a nursing home was when I was seven on a field trip with school. I thought everything felt really weird. A few years later, from stories on Facebook and the newspaper in my hometown in Arkansas, I saw how Ruby was spreading kindness in nursing homes. Ruby was showing me that these nursing homes were full of real people with even more real feelings.

I was just an elementary school kid when Ruby and I met by chance. She saw potential in me I didn't know I had. She asked me to be a part of the Three Wishes for Ruby's Residents team and I jumped at the chance to get involved. When I joined, I learned from Ruby that making others feel happy made me experience happiness too.

That was the first time I realized that you don't have to be a grown-up to make a difference, as I had never heard of any kid success stories like hers. From early on, I had learned by example from my parents to be kind in every way I can. Even when I was really little, we always tried to make an effort to help people less fortunate than us.

Fast-forward a few months. I had completed several projects with Ruby and the other members of the organization. We would have brainstorming sessions to come up with new ideas and projects to bring joy. Sometimes we did simple things like a Vienna Sausage Day (I don't know why Vienna sausages are so amazing, but it seems to be a universal truth they are the best sausages out there, according to our residents). And sometimes we did bigger projects.

The thing I'm most proud of was the Birthday Project. Early in my involvement, I was thinking about my upcoming birthday when I realized I didn't know how the residents spend their birthdays. When I asked my mom and found out pretty much nothing special happened, I quickly decided that would no longer be the case. Every month after that (until the COVID-19 pandemic), I would ask the nursing home staff for a list of everyone with a birthday that month, and then I would write a personalized birthday card for each one. In the middle of every month, we held a party with treats like cake, drinks, snacks, ice cream, and Happy Meals, and I even learned to play "Happy Birthday" on the piano so I could play it at each party.

Another project that I led was the Pillow Project. In a brainstorming session, someone said that they noticed that the pillows in the nursing homes didn't look very comfy, they looked like cardboard. We all talked about how each of us had a special pillow we couldn't sleep without, and that sparked the idea for this project. I volunteered to lead the effort. We ordered the pillows, had them delivered, put each one in a new pillowcase, and bagged them all up for transport to the nursing homes. We spent a whole day delivering pillows and hugs to every resident in each of the two nursing homes. That was the first project that really opened my eyes to how easy it was to be kind and how making the residents happy made me happy too. One lady even cried over her new pillow.

I'm now thirteen and live in South Carolina, where we're working on starting our own Three Wishes chapter. We're looking for the perfect nursing home to take action on once again. Looking back, Ruby and the Three Wishes organization have brought so much into my life and taught me so many valuable lessons. If I could make this much of a difference at a young age, I know you can too. Being kind isn't a chore, it's a reward!

BECKY MATHIS

Hi! I'm Becky Mathis and I teach 5th- and 6th-grade art at Harrison Middle School in Harrison, Arkansas. My favorite types of art projects include anything colorful and interesting. Students at HMS learn about many different art techniques and the elements of art while making fun projects that they can share with others. We display the work in the school's hallways. After a few weeks, I take the work down to return to the students. Last year, we began sharing our artwork with some of the area nursing homes through Three Wishes for Ruby's Residents organization. What an amazing experience that was!

Students loved the idea of upcycling their art, whether it be watercolor, acrylic paint, pastel, or collage, knowing it would be displayed beautifully and have such a positive impact. Many wrote letters describing themselves and what they enjoyed, while others created beautiful messages of kindness on their artwork. Often, elderly individuals imagine that they are receiving a gift from their own children or grandchildren.

Spreading kindness to seniors in your community by making art or writing letters or thoughtful words is a powerful action that gives you a voice, builds your confidence in making a difference, and impacts your world in a positive way. It's also fun and easy! What's really cool is seeing the photos or videos of residents receiving their artwork. You wouldn't believe how happy it makes them. Sometimes all it takes is a few kind words and a colorful art piece to bring tears of joy to another person. What you give to an area senior may be the only bright spot in their day. Realizing how amazing you can make someone else feel makes you feel good too!

A few simple projects you could create include painting rocks with bright colors, painting happy landscapes, making a flower collage, or even creating 3D art such as using colored tissue paper to make a flower arrangement. Another idea is for a group of students or the whole class to work together to create a larger mural for display in the residence hallways or common areas. There are many different mural art project ideas available on the Internet.

Kids really can make a difference and Three Wishes for Ruby's Residents is a great place to start!

ARSH PAL

I am Arsh Pal and I am twelve years old and from Dubuque, Iowa. I started my journey when I was eight years old through ArtByArsh. And one of my biggest inspirations was nursing home residents.

My mother works in a nursing home as an occupational therapist. Occasionally, I would go with her to work during the holidays. I used to visit, play therapy-related games, and talk to the residents during my visits. The smile and joy that I saw when the seniors were doing simple activities like talking inspired me to continue to help someone who is in need by doing small deeds for them.

During my journey, I came across Ruby and her inspirational work with nursing home residents. Our goals and motives were similar. Gradually, I became part of this wonderful organization, Three Wishes for Ruby's Residents, as an art advisor.

As a kid board member of the Loukoumi Foundation, an organization that's dedicated to making a difference in people's lives, I participated in their good deed day in November 2021. When I provided a list of items to Ruby for the residents, she created an Amazon wish list with all the items I had asked for. I was able to collect snacks, winter accessories, and activity items for the residents. Ruby also sent boxes of individually packed cookies with beautiful gift bags. I collected even more items through friends, family, and neighbors. My brother, Yuvan, and I donated all the items to the residents for that good deed day.

On my twelfth birthday in 2022, I wanted to do something special. I decided to celebrate my birthday with residents of a senior community in Dubuque. There were about fifteen residents who had birthdays in January. I collaborated with Ruby and executed Ruby's Resident's Card Project, where requests are sent via social media to provide birthday cards for nursing home residents. I received more than forty birthday cards from all over the country, which included some fun facts about that person or their state along with birthday wishes. Also, I have asked friends and family members to create birthday cards or send birthday wishes to the residents. I approached my brother Yuvan's kindergarten teacher to see if they could help in creating birthday cards too. I was amazed to see Yuvan coming home with handmade birthday wishes for the residents from the entire class. And Ruby sent birthday cakes.

On my birthday I was accompanied by my family and went to the facility with birthday balloons, cake, cupcakes, and birthday cards. The residents were eagerly waiting for me to come and celebrate my birthday with them. I read all the birthday cards and handed them over to the residents as a keepsake. They were delighted to see birthday cards from five-year-olds as well as from strangers from all over the country.

I have faced many challenges during these projects. As small or simple as it sounds (like making requests of family and friends to make cards or collect items for donations), it is not always easy. Sending reminders for deadlines and follow-ups to complete simple activities can be very time-consuming. However, the effort is worth it in the end, especially when you see the smiles and receive hugs from the residents. Even though they are small deeds, they are very powerful and impactful. They are touching someone's heart.

Ruby has touched many hearts through her service and I am one of them. Yuvan and I feel very proud to be a part of this wonderful organization.

The world needs more kindness and we all have the power to change the world by doing small, kind activities.

DELANEY REDDELL

My name is Delaney Reddell and I am twelve years old. I live in Newton County, Arkansas, and I'm a kid board member and youth director for literacy for Three

Wishes for Ruby's Residents.

As a youth activist, I make it my responsibility to bridge the generational gap between the young and old. I do this by communicating, giving, caring, loving, and making sure that seniors know they are valued and important. I have granted many wishes, but one of my favorites was when my family and I, along with other volunteers, created a garden for the nursing home residents of Newton County. Many of the residents once grew their own gardens and missed being able to harvest their vegetables. Growing a garden felt so good and it was great to do something that made a difference!

On occasion, some of the kids from my church go with me to the nursing home and we sing to the residents. This is so much fun because I love to sing! Three Wishes for Ruby's Residents also hosts Lunch Brunches at some of the local nursing facilities. We enjoy food together and the opportunity to meet the residents. I remember a Lunch Brunch where I met a kind, sweet, and loving lady named BethAnne. She reminded me to never, ever forget my roots and to always keep God first in my life. Conversations with seniors like BethAnne inspire me and make me want to be a better person and not take my youth for granted. To see seniors smile

makes me not only smile but also fills me with joy and happiness because I know that I made an impact on someone.

Another one of my favorite things to do is speaking on behalf of Three Wishes for Ruby's Residents. It is exciting to inform people about the simple and inexpensive things that they can do for seniors.

In my recent title holding as Princess of America–Miss Arkansas Superstar and Miss University of Arkansas-Diamond State Princess, I am able to promote Three Wishes for Ruby's Residents as part of my platform. I hope to one day reign as Miss Arkansas Outstanding Teen and Miss Arkansas, and I plan to promote and share this remarkable organization more throughout the state and the whole wide world.

Dr. Martin Luther King Jr. once said, "Life's most persistent and urgent question is, 'What are you doing for others?'" I feel being involved with this great organization has made me a wiser youth and is preparing me to be a better citizen in the future.

It is an honor to have joined Ruby on this amazing journey of changing the world, one senior and youth at a time!

4
Recipes from the Heart

Food, Stories & Memories

I've met so many seniors who love to cook. They really enjoy telling stories about food and sharing their cherished recipes. And sometimes their wish is just to have someone to talk to or share their recipes with. That's what puts a smile on their face. That is how they know they are not forgotten.

I LOVE
SECRET, OLD
RECIPES.

I mentioned cooking as a vintage skill earlier in the book. In this chapter, we can practice cooking with a few of the recipes that my senior friends have shared with me. I can't think of a better way to carry on someone's memory than through old recipes and meals. It's almost like a little piece of them gets to live forever.

I am not a chef, but I love to cook and I really love making my favorite things. Do you have a favorite meal that a relative makes on special occasions? I do. My great-grandmother made a Coca-Cola cake when I was a little girl. I have since learned to make it myself and now I think about her each time I do. I am lucky because I still have her original recipe on a card in her handwriting. It is like a piece of my great-grandmother is still with me and it's something that will be in my family forever.

I chose the following recipes because they are delicious and easy to make. I can imagine that they could become a tradition in your own family. I also chose them because the recipes came from a special nursing home senior who made an impact on my life.

Have a family member help you purchase the ingredients and make the recipe for your own special occasion. I promise you will love and cherish the time you spend baking with your family members and they will love the experience of cooking, too.

I hope that you enjoy these recipes and that you discover even more from the wonderful seniors in your life. I would love to hear about how well the recipes turned out for you. Send us an email at 3wishesforruby@gmail.com.

Dorothy's Cola Cake

Dorothy (aka GiGi) was born in 1919 and she was my first nursing home patient. She was also my great-grandmother. GiGi was a retired nurse. She loved animals, church, and socializing. She was a friend to everyone who knew her. She cooked a lot and she loved to host parties. She made the best chocolate cake in the world. She also had a huge sweet tooth. Her cola cake is delicious and it's one of my favorite desserts. I also think it might be more delicious because I think of my great-grandmother when we bake it.

CAKE INGREDIENTS

2 cups all-purpose flour

1 teaspoon baking soda

2 cups granulated sugar

½ cup butter

½ cup vegetable oil

½ cup cocoa powder

1 cup cola

½ cup buttermilk

2 eggs

1 teaspoon vanilla extract

1½ cups mini marshmallows

ICING INGREDIENTS

½ cup butter

6 tablespoons cocoa powder

6 tablespoons cola

3½ cups powdered sugar

1 teaspoon vanilla extract

1) Preheat the oven to 350°F.

2) For the cake, in a large bowl, sift the flour, baking soda, and granulated sugar together. Heat the butter, oil, cocoa, and cola in a saucepan over medium heat and stir until smooth and warm. Pour into the dry mix and stir until smooth. Add the buttermilk, eggs, and vanilla. Stir until smooth, then add the marshmallows and stir until they are mixed in well. Pour into a greased and floured 9"× 13" × 2" pan. Bake for 45 minutes or until a toothpick inserted into the center comes out clean.

3) For the icing, heat and stir the butter, cocoa, and cola in a saucepan over medium heat until smooth. Remove from the heat. Add the powdered sugar and vanilla. Stir until smooth and pour over the cake.

Mrs. Pearl's Chicago-style Pizza

Pearl was born as "Rose Elizabeth" in Italy in 1935. She eventually made her way to Chicago, Illinois, and she spent most of her life there. I called her "Pearl" and she had an unbelievable impact on my life; she is what inspired me to start the Three Wishes Project. One of her wishes was a Chicago-style pizza, which is pretty impossible to find in my small town. My mom and I decided to make her a pizza and we knocked it out of the ballpark. It definitely received Pearl's seal of approval. Here's the recipe. I hope you will think about her when you make the pizza and give a little shout to this amazing woman!

Leave out the pepperoni if you want to make it a veggie pizza.

INGREDIENTS

2 packages refrigerated pizza dough

14-ounce can or jar of your favorite pizza sauce

4 ounces pepperoni slices (optional)

2 cups shredded mozzarella cheese

1) Preheat the oven to 375°F.

2) Press the pizza dough into the bottom and sides of a very well-greased 9" × 12" baking sheet.

3) Cover the dough with the pizza sauce.

4) Evenly layer the pepperoni on top of the sauce, if using.

5) Cover with the cheese.

6) Bake, covered, for 25 minutes and then uncover and bake for 5 to 10 minutes to brown the top.

Momma's Famous Macaroni & Cheese

I've met a lot of nursing home residents named Ruby! This Ruby was an amazing cook, and she had over thirty grandchildren! Cooking was her hobby. I'm sharing her "secret" recipe. She said that as she got older she mostly wanted to make recipes that would make the great-grandkids and grandkids happy. She would always include this macaroni and cheese dish at any family get-togethers. You may never want any other kind of macaroni and cheese again after you try it. She said she never had a grandkid who didn't want seconds! She also said it was the only dish that never had anything left for leftovers!

INGREDIENTS

1 pound (4 cups dry) elbow macaroni noodles

2 cans evaporated milk (24 ounces total)

3 tablespoons butter

1 cup chicken broth

⅓ cup all-purpose flour

¾ cup grated Parmesan cheese

1 tablespoon Dijon mustard

Salt and pepper to taste

4½ cups shredded cheddar cheese

1) Boil the pasta until tender and drain.

2) Heat the milk, butter, and chicken broth in a large saucepan until melted and warm. Whisk in the flour until smooth. Boil on low for 3 minutes until it thickens slightly. Add the Parmesan cheese, mustard, salt, and pepper. Turn off the heat. Add the cheddar cheese and pasta. Stir well and serve!

Crockpot Casserole

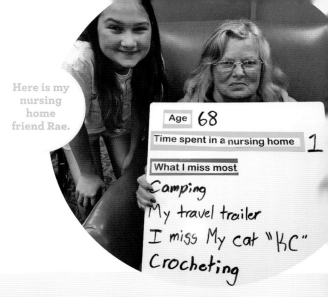

Here is my nursing home friend Rae.

Age 68

Time spent in a nursing home 1

What I miss most

Camping
My travel trailer
I miss My cat "KC"
Crocheting

Rae is one of my Ruby's Residents. She is in her seventies and she loved to cook for her family. She also liked to travel the country in her camper with her husband and her cat, K.C. She says that her family always asked her to cook this dish and she served cornbread on the side. She thinks it was the most popular recipe in her family and the one she prepared the most. Rae even knew the recipe by heart! Be sure to check out the cornbread recipe next!

INGREDIENTS

2 large baking potatoes, sliced into medallions

1 small onion, chopped

4 large carrots, sliced

1 pound cooked and drained hamburger meat

1 can green peas, drained

2 tablespoons butter

1 can tomato soup

1 can water

Salt and pepper to taste

1) Place the ingredients in layers in a large crockpot. Place the potatoes first, onion, carrots, hamburger meat, and green peas in one layer on top of the other. Cut the butter into slices and place on top. Cover with the soup and water.

2) Cover and cook on low for 4 to 6 hours or until the potatoes are tender. Season with salt and pepper.

3) Rae suggests serving with a side of cornbread muffins!

Lynda's Cornbread

My grandmother Lynda makes the best cornbread in the universe. It will go perfectly with Rae's Crockpot Casserole on page 99. It's a vintage skill. I believe everyone on the planet should know how to make good cornbread!

INGREDIENTS

1 cup cornmeal mix

1 cup self-rising flour

1 tablespoon sugar

1 teaspoon baking powder

1 cup buttermilk

1 egg, beaten

3 tablespoons vegetable oil

1) Preheat the oven to 375°F.

2) Mix all the ingredients, except for the oil, together in a large bowl.

3) For a pan of cornbread, pour the oil into the bottom of a 9" x 11" baking pan. Spread the oil out evenly and pour the batter on top. Bake for 35 minutes or until a toothpick inserted into the center comes out clean.

4) For cornbread muffins, use the oil to cover the bottom of each cup in a muffin pan. Fill each muffin cup two-thirds full with the batter. Bake for 30 minutes or until a toothpick inserted into the center of each comes out clean.

THIS IS LYNDA AND RAYMOND. THEY EACH HAVE A RECIPE TO SHARE.

Cowboy Peach Pie

Raymond is a real-life cowboy. He can train the wildest of horses. His peach pie is easy and super delicious! Raymond says this is a great recipe to make for a friend, parent, or loved one on special occasions!

INGREDIENTS

1 can of 12 biscuits

2 cans of peach pie filling

⅓ cup sugar

¼ cup butter

1) Preheat the oven to 375°F.

2) Roll each of the biscuits out on a floured surface until nice and thin like a pancake.

3) Place half the biscuits to cover the bottom of a greased deep-dish pie pan.

4) Cover the biscuits with the peach pie filling. Cover the peach filling with the remaining rolled biscuit dough.

5) Sprinkle the sugar evenly over the top of the dough. Slice the butter into pats and place on top of the sugar.

6) Bake for 20 minutes or until the top is lightly browned.

Chocolate Gravy

Marilyn is my helper at the nursing home. She is my eyes and ears and she lets me know if any of the seniors need something. She tells me if someone is admitted without shoes or if a person is out of cat food. Marilyn loves to cook and she misses being able to cook. Nearly eighty years old, she has cooked an awful lot of dishes in her long lifetime. She said her favorite thing to eat is chocolate gravy. Who knew? It's not quite what you think. It's mildly sweet but when you put this stuff on top of a biscuit, it might just be the best thing around. You know the best part? The kitchen staff in her nursing home makes the dish for her on special occasions like birthdays and Christmas! I hope you think of my friend Marilyn when you make her chocolate gravy. You can tell people all about her!

INGREDIENTS

½ cup sugar

2 tablespoons all-purpose flour

1 tablespoon cocoa powder

1½ cups milk

1 teaspoon vanilla extract

1) Mix all the ingredients together in a saucepan and stir constantly over medium heat until thick.

2) Serve over hot biscuits with butter.

Here's a little more about Marilyn!

Age 75

Time spent in a nursing home

What I miss most about my former Life

being able to cook
My pet
My Home life
Every day Chores
Holidays at h

Banana Pancakes

This is one of my favorite recipes to make for my mom on a special day. It's easy to make and we usually have these ingredients lying around the house anyhow. The lady who shared it with me is Margaret and she has lived in the nursing home for a very long time. She had not made a home-cooked meal in years but she was smiling so big when she shared this recipe with me. It brought back great memories of her cooking for her family. Margaret is in her nineties! She was born in 1924. I asked her what was the great invention of her lifetime and she had a hard time choosing. There were so many things she could choose from—washing machine, dishwasher, Hershey's chocolate bar, refrigerator—she ultimately chose the air conditioner. She said it was like a miracle having your house cooled in the summer heat!

INGREDIENTS

1 cup all-purpose flour

2 tablespoons sugar

2 teaspoons baking powder

¼ teaspoon salt

1 egg, beaten

2 tablespoons vegetable oil

1 cup milk or buttermilk

2 ripe bananas, mashed

1) Combine the flour, sugar, baking powder, and salt in a small bowl and mix well.

2) In a separate large bowl, mix together the egg, oil, milk, and bananas.

3) Mix the dry ingredients into the wet ingredients and stir, leaving the mixture a little lumpy so you have some good pieces of banana in the batter.

4) Heat an oiled frying pan over medium heat. Pour ⅓ cup of batter for each pancake. Flip when bubbles start to form in the center of the pancake. Cook until golden brown on the other side. Makes about 10 pancakes.

Turkey Dressing

I feel like I have known Retha my whole life. She is ninety-seven years old as of this writing. One of the fondest stories of her life revolves around chickens. She lived with her husband in Kansas City, Missouri, while he completed dental school. This was during the time of World War II and times were hard. Retha did all she could to keep the family fed and part of that involved getting butchered beef for free from her family's farm and canning it for her family to eat for months. The super funny part was when Retha's father decided the couple might like some fresh chickens from the farm. The dad loaded up a gunnysack full of live chickens, got on a train, and headed to surprise her in Kansas City. The dad hadn't thought this out too much because Retha and her husband lived in an apartment building at the time and didn't have a place to prepare the chickens to eat! They were about to waste the food, so they decided to pluck the chickens in the apartment bathtub! Back in these days, most apartment complexes had incinerators in the basements, so that is exactly where all the unwanted parts of the chicken went that day. It wasn't long until everyone in the complex wondered what the awful smell was! Their little fiasco was top secret but they did have chicken to last them for months! Here's a recipe from Retha that the whole family loved.

Retha on her ninety-seventh birthday in 2022. Her turkey dressing recipe is one of the best things ever!

INGREDIENTS

3 cups chopped onion

3 cups chopped celery

1 cup unsalted butter

1 tablespoon olive oil

1 skillet of cornbread (use your favorite cornbread mix or try Lynda's Cornbread on page 100, crumbled)

10 slices toast or biscuits, broken into pieces

3 cups turkey stock

½ to 1 cup chopped fresh sage

½ teaspoon pepper

2 eggs, beaten

1) Preheat the oven to 350°F.

2) In a large pot, sauté the onion and celery in the butter and olive oil for about 7 minutes.

3) Add the cornbread and toast or biscuits to the pot.

4) Add the turkey stock as needed to form the right consistency (similar to pudding). Add the sage and pepper to your taste. Add the eggs.

5) Pour the mixture into a 9" x 13" casserole dish and place into the oven.

6) Bake, covered, for 20 to 30 minutes.

Easy Baked Chicken Fried Steak

Here I am with Mary, the famous "Cheese Lady."

I know I am not supposed to have favorites but sometimes I can't help it. Mary is one of my favorite residents of all time. She and I made a video with CBS News in 2019 and the video went viral with millions of views! In the video, Mary tells me she misses real cheese and I buy her some. She became widely known as "The Cheese Lady" and if you are lucky enough to receive a letter from her, she will sign it, "Love, The Cheese Lady." One time I asked her what her family wanted her to cook the most during her lifetime. She didn't hesitate to say, "Chicken fried steak." She learned to bake it in the oven because frying became a little difficult for her over the years. She says the baked version is way better and way easier.

INGREDIENTS

½ cup all-purpose flour

2 teaspoons salt

1 teaspoon pepper

⅔ cup Italian bread crumbs

3 egg whites

3 tablespoons milk

4 to 6 cube steaks (tenderized is best)

2 packages white country gravy mix

1) Preheat the oven to 400°F. Spray a sheet pan with nonstick spray. Combine the flour, salt, pepper, and bread crumbs in a bowl and mix.

2) In a separate bowl, beat the egg whites and milk together. Dip one cube steak into the flour mixture first. Next, dip the cube steak in the egg mixture. Dip it in the flour mixture one more time. Place on the baking sheet.

3) Repeat the steps for the remaining steaks. Place the pan in the oven and bake for 10 minutes.

4) Turn the steaks over and bake for another 10 minutes. Make the gravy according to the package instructions and serve on top or on the side with the steaks.

Zucchini Bread

OK. Don't let the name fool you because it really fooled me. This recipe sounds awful and I'm not sure I would have ever eaten it if sweet Henrietta had not put me on the spot one day in the nursing home. She grew the zucchini in the garden and had her family bring in all the ingredients to make the bread. She spent most of the day in the physical therapy department's kitchen making this concoction and this happened to be the day I visited Henrietta. The bread was still warm and she offered my mom and me a piece. I was never going to say no, but, on the inside, I was scared that I was going to hate it. I took a bite right in front of her and I was prepared to give the act of my life, but to my surprise it was delicious. I asked for another one! I still wonder to this day if it actually had zucchini inside but she swears it did. You bake it and let me know what you think!

INGREDIENTS

3 cups grated fresh zucchini

3 cups all-purpose flour

1 teaspoon baking soda

1 teaspoon baking powder

2 teaspoons ground cinnamon

½ teaspoon ground ginger

½ teaspoon ground nutmeg

1 cup granulated sugar

½ cup brown sugar

2 large eggs, beaten

2 teaspoons vanilla extract

¾ cup butter, melted

1 cup chopped pecans

1) Preheat the oven to 350°F.

2) Let the grated zucchini sit out, drying slightly, while you prepare the rest of the recipe.

3) In a large bowl, whisk together the flour, baking soda, baking powder, cinnamon, ginger, and nutmeg.

4) In another large bowl, whisk together the sugars, eggs, and vanilla. Stir in the drained grated zucchini and then the melted butter.

5) Add the flour mixture, a little at a time, to the sugar-egg-zucchini mixture and stir until mixed well. Stir in the nuts last.

6) Divide the batter equally and pour into two greased and floured loaf pans.

7) Bake for 50 minutes.

A WORD FROM MOM

MY NAME IS AMANDA CHITSEY and I am Ruby's mom. The question I am asked most often is, "How did Ruby turn out this way?" I mean, Ruby has accomplished a lot. Her resume is three pages long and it is honestly more impressive than most adults' I know. How does a child do something so special that it ends up being honored by the likes of Prince Harry and Chelsea Clinton? And what is equally important to me as a parent is the question that I am not asked, "How did you raise a happy child?"

I give three things credit for Ruby's accomplishments and happiness. First, and probably the most obvious, is the fact that I manage nursing homes for a living. It is no surprise that Ruby's exposure to my work impacted her life in some way. But yet, my sons had the same exposure, and they did not respond in the way that Ruby did. It's just that she really loves the older generation. Ruby indeed grew up inside nursing homes. I'd venture to say that my children have probably spent more time inside nursing homes than just about any other kids on the planet and, for Ruby, it became a true source of happiness.

With three children it has always amazed me how they are each so very different. My oldest son seemed invincible from birth or at least I'd like to describe him as having a bulletproof veil. He was fearless when he began to walk and each step was careless and taken without fear or thought. Ruby took her steps much differently as she began to crawl and walk. It appeared as though each of her steps was planned out carefully and taken with such caution that it was as if she were savoring each beautiful step and equally confident that each step would not lead to a fall.

Ruby's thoughtful approach to life only grew stronger as she got older. I noticed that her take on the world was unique compared to her siblings and other children around her. When I presented my boys with a new toy truck or if they accomplished something new, like making their first hit off the tee, they would be triumphant and anyone could see the joy on their faces. When Max, my smallest, learned to swim, it was absolutely the best day of his life. Ruby, on the other hand, was way more reserved and harder to elicit true joy. Her reactions to life's typical childhood

WE LOVE TO SHOP FOR SENIORS.

accomplishments were beautifully subdued and, at times, absent. The things that brought most kids joy didn't seem to stir a reaction in Ruby. Give her a doll and she would look at you like you were from another planet; let her save a cicada or make a friend happy, and she would beam like the sun itself for days.

Ruby was born with certain traits and instincts that I can't take any credit for. I describe her as having a giant heart and I credit this as being the second part of what led to her success. Ruby's heart is her superpower. Can a giant heart be both a blessing and a curse? Yes, it

can. Ruby saw and felt every little thing around her. This all started because as a ten-year-old at work with her mother, she noticed a senior staring too long out a window. What ten-year-old sees that? How many kids would notice that small detail, much less act on it?

Ruby has vision and she sees and feels things in her world that most of us don't. What makes it successful for her is the action behind her vision. I saw Ruby speak at a FedEx conference about kindness when she was nine years old. There wasn't a dry eye in the room. She moved them with her heart and it was one of the most powerful things I have ever seen. Her authenticity and sincerity are palpable in the way she moves, hugs, speaks, and smiles. It's a gift and it's difficult for me to describe the way she is able to touch someone's soul so deeply. I don't pretend to understand it completely, but it is most certainly a huge factor in her success and happiness.

Lastly, I think our parenting style impacted Ruby in a positive way. We saw that Ruby wasn't going to be happy with the more popular kid activities and extracurriculars that were readily available to us in a small town. Instead of forcing her to do the things that every other kid was doing or allow her to have no extracurriculars at all, we helped Ruby carve her own path. It was hard. Life would have been much easier if she liked to dance because the world is made for our children to immerse themselves in these types of activities. At a very early age, we wanted Ruby's voice and opinions to matter.

Ruby showed me the world from her perspective and it was beautifully simple. She let me see the plight and life of nursing home seniors through the eyes of a child. That alone changed my career forever. We sought out opportunities for her to use her voice as young as age nine. We paid attention to the moments in life that made her happiest and we tried to find ways that she could re-create that happiness on her own.

Ruby helped the nursing home seniors for sure, but they helped her just as much. They solidly reinforced to her what we had already said time and time again: "You have a superpower, Ruby." They gave her the confidence to share it with the world. This is perhaps our greatest gift to Ruby, to have preserved her giant heart in a world that can be quite cold, and allowed it to stay on course, untarnished, and remain the positive force that it is.

My advice to any parent is to listen and observe your child as they go about their daily little lives. What makes them tick? What drives them? I remind myself constantly that I only get twelve summers with my kids in my house. I will get to drive them to that glorious "first day of school" ten times if I'm very lucky. Will they leave after that eighteenth birthday celebration? Probably. My hope is that I have given them each the tools and vision they need to create their own little box of "happiness" that they can carry with them wherever they go.

Happiness doesn't just come to us. We make it ourselves and for our family. It comes from finding joy in the simple things that are right before us.

ACKNOWLEDGMENTS

I can't possibly list all of the people who helped make this book come to life. I would surely leave out someone special if I tried and that would break my heart into pieces.

Let me just acknowledge all of my senior nursing home friends, past and present, for sharing their lives with me for all these years. Each of you will always be a part of me.

I would also like to thank the staff of the nursing homes for trusting me and always being kind. I see your hard work and I have mad respect for the warriors who work in long-term care. Y'all are my heroes.

I would like to thank Valley Springs School for loving me and for being the best school ever.

Thanks to Chasey Hudson, photography student at Harrison High School, for the photos.

I would like to thank GoFundMe for believing in me and for giving me a platform to share my cause with the world.

I would like to thank Steve Hartman and his cameraman, Bob, for showing the world what I do.

Got to thank my mom for always seeing the hero inside of me.

OTHER BOOKS FROM OUR TOMORROW
A BOOK SERIES WRITTEN BY YOUNG COMMUNITY LEADERS AND ACTIVISTS, DEDICATED TO INSPIRING, UPLIFTING, AND EMPOWERING THE NEXT GENERATION OF LEADERS

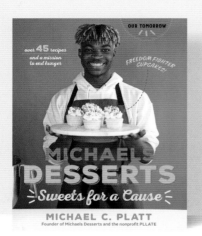

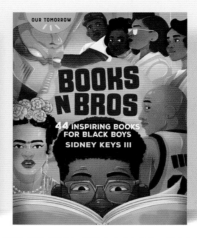

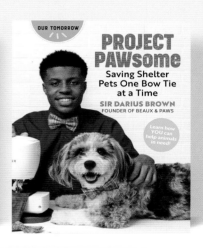

Michaels Desserts
Sweets for a Cause

Michael Platt

A fun cookbook for all ages by teen baker, social entrepreneur, and food justice advocate Michael C. Platt, inspired by his mission to end food insecurity one dessert at a time. Recipes include No Kid Hungry French Toast Breakfast Cupcakes, Nelson Mandela Malva Pudding Cupcakes, and Booker T. Washington Vegan Chocolate Cupcakes.

ISBN 9781684620470

Books N Bros
44 Inspiring Books for Black Boys

Sidney Keys III

From teen entrepreneur and literacy advocate Sidney Keys III, a reading guide that centers on Black boys, inspired by the success of his book club Books N Bros. Featured books include *Hidden Figures: Young Readers' Edition* by Margot Lee Shetterly, *Black Boy White School* by Brian F. Walker, and *Shuri: A Black Panther Novel* by Nic Stone.

ISBN 9781684620487

Project PAWsome
Saving Shelter Pets One Bow Tie at a Time

Sir Darius Brown

Teen social entrepreneur Sir Darius Brown tells how his company Beaux & Paws uses bow ties to help pets in animal shelters get adopted quicker—and how readers can get involved with local shelters themselves. Includes heartwarming stories and photos of dozens of dogs Sir Darius has saved, plus instructions for how to make your own bow ties.

ISBN 9781684620708